National Standards & Guidelines
For Physical Education Teacher Education
3rd Edition

National Association for Sport and Physical Education
an association of the American Alliance for Health, Physical Education, Recreation and Dance

Revised by:

Initial Physical Education Teacher Education Standards Task Force,
National Association for Sport and Physical Education

Advanced Physical Education Teacher Education Standards Task Force,
National Association for Sport and Physical Education

Principal writers for this edition:

Tabatha Uhrich, Towson University

Stevie Chepko, Winthrop University

Lynn Couturier, State University of New York, Cortland

To order more copies of this book (stock # 304-10460):

Web: www.naspeinfo.org
E-mail: customerservice@aahperd.org
Phone: (800) 321-0789; (412) 741-1288 outside the United States
Fax: (412) 741-0609
Mail: AAHPERD Publications Fulfillment Center
        P.O. Box 1020, Sewickley, PA 15143-1020

ISBN: 978-0-88314-931-7
Printed in the United States

ACKNOWLEDGEMENTS

In summer 2006, the National Association for Sport and Physical Education (NASPE) appointed task forces to revise both the 2001 Initial and Advanced Physical Education Teacher Education Standards. Both task forces owe a debt of gratitude to the committees that went before them for their excellent work, and to NASPE liaison De Raynes for her tireless efforts on behalf of the project. Task force members also send their gratitude to all the professionals in the field who participated in reviewing drafts of the documents. We believe that these standards are stronger because of the input from so many professionals.

Initial Physical Education Teacher Education Standards Task Force (Chapters 1 & 2)

Stevie Chepko (Task Force Chair), Winthrop University
Lynn Couturier, State University of New York, Cortland
Gibson Darden, Coastal Carolina University
Bonnie Doyle, Portland (Oregon) Public Schools
Ritchie Gabbei, Western Illinois University
Tabatha Uhrich, Towson University

Advanced Physical Education Teacher Education Standards Task Force (Chapter 3)

Mandi Anderson (Task Force Chair), Iowa State University
Bryan McCullick, University of Georgia
Beverly Mitchell, Kennesaw State University

De Raynes, NASPE liaison

TABLE OF CONTENTS

PREFACE

Periodically, the National Association for Sport and Physical Education (NASPE) appoints task forces to review and revise its National Standards for Initial and Advanced Physical Education Teacher Education (PETE). The charge to each task force: Review the current standards, examine the existing literature and pedagogical research, analyze current best practices in teaching and recommend revisions for each set of standards. The two task forces charged with revising the 2001 standards began their work in October 2006.

The task forces spent two years completing the revision process. After an extensive literature review and much discussion about critical knowledge, skills and dispositions at each level, the task forces developed drafts for new standards and made them available for targeted and public review. The public review included stakeholders in the standards process, including PETE faculty members, K-12 practitioners, administrators (college and K-12) and representatives of other specialized professional associations. The task forces drafted and revised iterations of the standards after each round of professional review and posted each set of standards on NASPE's Web site for member comment.

In addition to the targeted review and electronic posting, sessions at the American Alliance for Health, Physical Education, Recreation and Dance (AAHPERD) 2007 and 2008 national conventions gave members opportunities to ask questions, provide feedback and offer suggestions. After multiple review cycles, the task forces presented the final documents to the NASPE Delegate Assembly for review and the NASPE Executive Board for final approval (Initial Standards, April 2007; Advanced Standards, March 2008).

The result of all that preparation, work and review, then, are PETE Standards that reflect the views and beliefs of dedicated professionals who are committed to improving teacher preparation programs at both the initial and advanced levels. Their willingness to ask questions and suggest recommendations has strengthened the standards greatly and allowed both task forces to make informed decisions.

These standards represent a comprehensive vision of what a physical education teacher should know and be able to do upon initial licensure (Initial Standards) and post-initial licensure, master's degree (Advanced Standards). The common elements in both sets of standards are a core commitment to creating a fair and equitable learning environment and the belief that all students can be physically educated. These dispositions form the foundation for professional behaviors that characterize a highly qualified teacher. Taken in their entirety, the Initial and Advanced PETE Standards form the infrastructure for a performance-based assessment system that requires initial and advanced teacher candidates to demonstrate the content and pedagogical knowledge, skills and dispositions that NASPE has identified as important.

CHAPTER 1

2008 National Standards for Initial Physical Education Teacher Education

Introduction to the Initial Standards

When NASPE's Initial Physical Education Teacher Education Standards task force first met in October 2006, members examined the existing standards, reviewed publications on current best practices in teaching and pedagogical research, and discussed the critical skills, knowledge and dispositions that should characterize physical education teachers entering their first year of teaching.

Because many professional preparation programs use NASPE's Initial PETE Standards to merit NASPE/ National Council for Accreditation of Teacher Education (NCATE) accreditation, the task force also considered the NASPE/NCATE review process throughout its work.

Although the new standards appear to be quite different from the 2001 standards, all of the earlier standards' essential knowledge, skills and dispositions remain. The task force strove to develop standards and elements (formerly "outcomes") that most teacher preparation programs could meet with the evidence, rigorous assessments and data that they already collect.

At the same time, the new standards do reflect a paradigm shift: toward thinking about physical education as a performance-based discipline, much like music, dance and art. Under the 2008 Standards, teacher preparation programs will need to assess teacher candidates' physical skills, performance concepts and health-related fitness, which are new expectations. The revised standards now number six (revised from 10) and feature 28 elements (revised from 44 outcomes). They reflect consensus among experienced physical educators at all levels as to what a beginning teacher should know, believe and be able to do.

The task force's discussions were informed by the Five Core Propositions that the National Board for Professional Teaching Standards (NBPTS, 2002) identified and the 10 Interstate New Teacher Assessment and Support Consortium (INTASC) Principles (1992). Although the revised standards are more closely aligned with the Five Core Propositions, one can find the content of the INTASC Principles in individual elements within the standards. *Examples*:

- Proposition 1: Teachers Are Committed to Students and Their Learning influenced the development of revised Standards 3, 4 and 6.

- Proposition 2: Teachers Know the Subjects They Teach and How to Teach Those Subjects to Students guided the task force in developing new Standard 2 on physical competency, and influenced the content of Standards 1 through 4.

- Proposition 3: Teachers Are Responsible for Managing and Monitoring Student Learning influenced Standards 3, 4 and 5.

- Proposition 4: Teachers Think Systematically About Their Practice and Learn From Experience aligns with Standard 5, in that it focuses on using assessment and developing candidates as reflective practitioners.

- Proposition 5: Teachers Are Members of Learning Communities most closely aligns with Standard 6, which is intended to develop teacher candidates as future professionals

Other documents that influenced the 2008 Initial Standards:

- *Moving Into the Future: National Standards for Physical Education* (NASPE, 2004).

- *Looking at Physical Education From a Developmental Perspective: A Guide to Teaching* (NASPE, 1995).

- *What Constitutes a Highly Qualified Physical Education Teacher?* (NASPE, 2007).

- "Expertise: The Wonder of Exemplary Performances" (Berliner, 1994).

- *The Wisdom of Practice: Essays on Teaching, Learning and Learning to Teach* (Shulman, 2004a, 2004b, 2004c).

- "What Knowledge Is of Most Worth? Perspectives on Kinesiology From Pedagogy" (Rink, 2007).

Rationale for Changes

The task force applied four guiding principles in its approach to revising the current standards:

1. Align the Initial PETE Standards with NASPE's 2004 K-12 National Standards for Physical Education.

2. Ensure that the revised PETE standards reflect the "best practices" of teacher education as found in the current literature.

3. Align the standards explicitly with NCATE Unit Standard 1, which requires candidates "… to know and demonstrate the content, pedagogical and professional knowledge, skills and dispositions necessary to help all students learn" (NCATE, 2008, p.12).

4. Include only those standards and elements that are measurable and achievable in an initial licensure program.

Performance-Based Discipline

Guided by Proposition 2 of NBPTS's Five Core Propositions (that teachers know the subjects they teach and know how to teach the subjects), the standard that requires teacher candidates to demonstrate competency in motor skills and movement patterns, along with achieving and maintaining a health-enhancing level of physical fitness, is new. NASPE believes that, as a performance-based discipline similar to dance, music, art and theater, motor competency/fitness is essential for teacher candidates, at least at the same level expected of students as they exit high school. While NASPE can prescribe assessment of motor competency, it's up to individual PETE programs to set standards of achievement for their teacher candidates, to define how those candidates are assessed, and to determine program benchmarks.

Over the past 10 years, PETE professionals have expressed increasing amounts of concern about the level of motor and fitness competency that candidates seeking admission to PETE programs display. Repeatedly, they've shared their concerns that too many candidates entering PETE programs lack competency in the fundamental movement skills of running, jumping, kicking, throwing, catching and striking. This lack of competency hinders candidates' ability to become competent teachers who can demonstrate and apply these skills effectively in a movement environment.

Adding his voice to the issue, Daryl Siedentop (2008) — professor emeritus at Ohio State University, who has written numerous articles and textbooks on physical education teacher education — says PETE programs have not made adequate provisions for content knowledge in K-3 skill themes, sport technique and tactics, and health-related activity and fitness. He also has documented a reduction in credit-hour requirements in motor competency for the most recent generation of PETE candidates, finding that PETE programs often require as few as nine credit hours of performance-based coursework, compared to 36 to 56 credit hours for dance and music programs.

Through feedback in open-forum discussions and during the process of drafting the Initial Standards, PETE professionals supported adding a motor-performance competency requirement. NASPE found that many university-based PETE programs already require their candidates to possess some competency in skill and fitness, so a precedent had been established.

Supporting Research

In a survey of 70 NCATE-approved PETE programs, Staffo and Stier (2000) found that, of the programs that had established a fitness requirement for teacher candidates, 78 percent had had the requirement in place between five and 20 years. Of the 50 program chairs responding, 49 agreed that "physical education majors seeking to become teachers should be physically fit and should project an image that promotes physical activity." Also, 76 percent agreed that "physical education departments have an obligation to assess the physical fitness levels of their majors" (p. 50). That research confirms previous research from Bandon and Evans (1988), Dotson (1988), Krause and Melville (1993) and Melville and Jones (1990).

As Siedentop (2008) further noted: "One of the concerns I have heard for many years is that PE units in schools are typically so short that students don't get a chance to be sufficiently competent in an activity to engage in it outside of class. My guess is that they are short because too many PE teachers have not been given the opportunity to develop the [content knowledge] necessary to take students beyond a rudimentary introduction to an activity." Creating a standard specific to movement and fitness competency is long overdue in the discipline. As do the performance-based disciplines of art, music and dance, physical education must ensure that teacher candidates are competent in their content area of human movement and fitness.

How the Standards Have Changed

In this revision, NASPE has reduced the number of standards from 10 to six, with a corresponding reduction in elements from 44 to 28. Most of the 28 elements are similar to the outcomes in the previous edition of the standards, but many have been aligned under new or different standards (see the Alignment Chart in Appendix A). The changes have affected primarily the former Standards 2 (Growth and Development), 3 (Diversity), 7 (Assessment), 8 (Reflection), 9 (Technology) and 10 (Collaboration).

The content of former Standard 2 (Growth and Development) is now contained in revised Standards 1, 3 and 4. The content of former Standard 3 (Diversity) now appears within seven elements under four different standards. That reflects NASPE's belief that meeting the needs of a diverse student population is fundamental to teaching; therefore, diversity should be present in a variety of standards and elements

This revision also has strengthened the commitment to professional dispositions. Standard 6 is devoted to this area, ensuring that teacher candidates will demonstrate the behaviors expected of effective teachers. NCATE's definition of Professional Dispositions (NCATE, 2008) provides the framework for the new Standard 6. The core belief that all students can learn is explicit in the standard, as is a commitment to creating a fair and equitable learning environment.

These new standards reduce the emphasis on teacher candidates' interactions with parents found in the 2001 Standard 10. Most PETE programs can provide only limited opportunities for teacher candidates to interact with parents, making this element difficult to document and assess.

NASPE has eliminated Standards 7 and 8 in this revision, but has included assessment and the reflective cycle in the new Standard 5 (Impact on Student Learning). NASPE also has eliminated Standards 9 and 10, but has included the use of technology to enhance student learning as part of Standard 3 and incorporated collaboration and professional development into Standard 6.

2008 NATIONAL STANDARDS
FOR INITIAL PHYSICAL EDUCATION TEACHER EDUCATION

These standards are intended to describe the minimal competencies expected of a beginning physical education teacher. Even experienced physical educators, however, can continually refresh their professional development by reviewing the standards and elements and evaluating their knowledge, skills and dispositions at the acceptable and target levels.

Note: Throughout the standards, elements and rubrics that follow, the term **teacher candidate(s)** refers to pre-service teachers in an initial preparation program.

Standard 1: Scientific and Theoretical Knowledge
Physical education teacher candidates know and apply discipline-specific scientific and theoretical concepts critical to the development of physically educated individuals.

Elements – Teacher candidates will:

1.1 Describe and apply physiological and biomechanical concepts related to skillful movement, physical activity and fitness.

1.2 Describe and apply motor learning and psychological/behavioral theory related to skillful movement, physical activity and fitness.

1.3 Describe and apply motor development theory and principles related to skillful movement, physical activity and fitness.

1.4 Identify historical, philosophical and social perspectives of physical education issues and legislation.

1.5 Analyze and correct critical elements of motor skills and performance concepts.

The intent is to identify critical foundational knowledge and to ensure that teacher candidates can apply that knowledge in an authentic setting. Note that three of the elements begin with "describe and apply," and one begins with "analyze and correct." Thus, knowledge tests such as state licensure tests or comprehensive exams won't provide sufficient evidence if teacher candidates are not required to demonstrate application of that knowledge.

Standard 2: Skill-Based and Fitness-Based Competence*
Physical education teacher candidates are physically educated individuals with the knowledge and skills necessary to demonstrate competent movement performance and health-enhancing fitness as delineated in the NASPE K–12 Standards.

Elements – Teacher candidates will:

2.1 Demonstrate personal competence in motor skill performance for a variety of physical activities and movement patterns.

2.2 Achieve and maintain a health-enhancing level of fitness throughout the program.

2.3 Demonstrate performance concepts related to skillful movement in a variety of physical activities.

* To avoid discrimination against those with disabilities, physical education teacher candidates with special needs are allowed and encouraged to use a variety of accommodations and/or modifications to demonstrate competent movement and performance concepts (modified/adapted equipment, augmented communication devices, multi-media devices, etc.) and fitness (weight-training programs, exercise logs, etc.).

The intent is to ensure that teacher candidates are themselves physically educated. They must be able to meet the same expectations that a physically educated high school senior would, as defined in the NASPE National Standards for Physical Education (2004). This will require teacher candidates to show competency in a variety of motor skills and performance concepts. (PETE programs have the flexibility to determine what defines competency.)

Assessment in these areas should include a wide range of skills, including fundamental motor patterns, as well as teacher candidates' ability to execute concepts and strategies in an authentic environment. Teacher candidates also must reach and maintain a health-enhancing level of personal fitness. (PETE program faculty members should determine for themselves what constitutes a health-enhancing level of fitness.) The phrase "achieve and maintain" indicates that assessment must occur at more than one point in a program.

Note: PETE programs should consider providing fitness-development programs for teacher candidates who need to improve their fitness levels. Program staff will need to develop a system of tracking teacher candidate performance for aspects of Standard 2, as well as establishing policies for accommodating those teacher candidates with documented disabilities.

Standard 3: Planning and Implementation
Physical education teacher candidates plan and implement developmentally appropriate learning experiences aligned with local, state and national standards to address the diverse needs of all students.

Elements – Teacher candidates will:

3.1 Design and implement short- and long-term plans that are linked to program and instruction goals, as well as a variety of student needs.

3.2 Develop and implement appropriate (e.g., measurable, developmentally appropriate, performance-based) goals and objectives aligned with local, state and/or national standards.

3.3 Design and implement content that is aligned with lesson objectives.

3.4 Plan for and manage resources to provide active, fair and equitable learning experiences.

3.5 Plan and adapt instruction for diverse student needs, adding specific accommodations and/or modifications for student exceptionalities.

3.6 Plan and implement progressive and sequential instruction that addresses the diverse needs of all students.

3.7 Demonstrate knowledge of current technology by planning and implementing learning experiences that require students to appropriately use technology to meet lesson objectives.

The intent is to emphasize the importance of planning for effective teaching. Planning must encompass short- and long-term plans, standards (national, state and local) and the diverse needs of students. Teacher candidates should consider progressions and adaptations in advance of executing the lesson. The planning does not occur in isolation ("design and implement," "plan and adapt"). Planning must be implemented to meet the standard's intent. Thus, if a lesson plan is used as evidence for this standard, the teacher candidate must execute the lesson in addition to planning it.

Standard 4: Instructional Delivery and Management
Physical education teacher candidates use effective communication and pedagogical skills and strategies to enhance student engagement and learning.

Elements – Teacher candidates will:

4.1 Demonstrate effective verbal and non-verbal communication skills across a variety of instructional formats.

4.2 Implement effective demonstrations, explanations and instructional cues and prompts to link physical activity concepts to appropriate learning experiences.

4.3 Provide effective instructional feedback for skill acquisition, student learning and motivation.

4.4 Recognize the changing dynamics of the environment and adjust instructional tasks based on student responses.

4.5 Use managerial rules, routines and transitions to create and maintain a safe and effective learning environment.

4.6 Implement strategies to help students demonstrate responsible personal and social behaviors in a productive learning environment.

The intent is to focus on lesson delivery. Therefore, elements center on communication, motivation and management. Teacher candidates should exhibit effective feedback and behavior-management skills, as well as being able to adapt to the changing instructional environment as the lesson progresses.

Standard 5: Impact on Student Learning
Physical education teacher candidates use assessments and reflection to foster student learning and inform decisions about instruction.

Elements – Teacher candidates will:

5.1 Select or create appropriate assessments that will measure student achievement of goals and objectives.

5.2 Use appropriate assessments to evaluate student learning before, during and after instruction.

5.3 Use the reflective cycle to implement change in teacher performance, student learning and/or instruction goals and decisions.

The intent is to consider the impact of the teacher candidate's instruction on student learning. Elements 5.1 and 5.2 highlight the importance of assessment to everything the teacher candidate does. Teacher candidates must be familiar with different forms of assessment and be able to develop their own assessments. Assessment must form an integral part of each lesson and must be used to guide instructional decisions and planning. Teacher candidates also must be reflective practitioners who critique their own performance, as well as their students' learning. The reflective cycle is not complete unless teacher candidates also use that information to adjust their instructional plans and/or improve their own teaching.

Standard 6: Professionalism
Physical education teacher candidates demonstrate dispositions that are essential to becoming effective professionals.

Elements – Teacher candidates will:

6.1 Demonstrate behaviors that are consistent with the belief that all students can become physically educated individuals.

6.2 Participate in activities that enhance collaboration and lead to professional growth and development.

6.3 Demonstrate behaviors that are consistent with the professional ethics of highly qualified teachers.

6.4 Communicate in ways that convey respect and sensitivity.

The intent is to consider those behaviors that constitute professionalism for teacher candidates. Teacher candidates are expected to demonstrate sensitivity and ethical behavior. They also must consider how they will engage in professional development and work with colleagues in the school system.

SAMPLE RUBRICS FOR INITIAL PETE STANDARDS

These rubrics are intended to guide program staff in understanding the acceptable level of candidate performance for meeting NASPE PETE Standards. They are not meant to be prescriptive in any way. PETE programs should develop their own rubrics specific to their assessments and aligned with the standards/elements to assess the performance of their teacher candidates. Programs should feel free to use as much of the language in these rubrics as is useful to their own purposes.

Standard 1: Scientific and Theoretical Knowledge
Physical education teacher candidates (TC) know and apply discipline-specific scientific and theoretical concepts critical to the development of physically educated individuals.

Element	Unacceptable	Acceptable	Target
1.1 Describe and apply physiological and biomechanical concepts related to skillful movement, physical activity and fitness.	TC applies physiological and biomechanical concepts in planning for and delivering instruction. Skill cues are appropriate in plan, but TC fails to use the identified skill cues during the lesson. TC instruction for skillful movement, physical activity or fitness is given using generalized terms and is concerned with the "how" of the movement, physical activity or fitness. TC fails to meet the criterion score established by the program on selected assessments in physiology and/or biomechanics.	TC applies physiological and biomechanical concepts appropriately in planning for and delivering instruction. Skill cues identified in the plan are used during the lesson. TC instruction for skillful movement, physical activities or fitness includes the "how" and "why" of the movement, physical activity or fitness. TC meets the criterion score established by the program on selected assessments in physiology and biomechanics.	TC applies physiological and biomechanical concepts appropriately in planning for and delivering instruction for all stages of student proficiency. Skill cues are identified in the plan and are used consistently during the lesson. TC instruction for skillful movement, physical activity or fitness includes the "how" and "why" of the movement, physical activity or fitness. TC exceeds the criterion score established by the program on selected assessments in physiology and biomechanics.
Element	Unacceptable	Acceptable	Target
1.2 Describe and apply motor learning and psychological/ behavioral theory related to skillful movement, physical activity and fitness.	TC demonstrates knowledge of the various theories but fails to apply theories to teaching. Practice conditions used for skill acquisition do not allow for individual differences. TC uses punitive measures to control behavior. TC fails to meet the criterion score established by the program on assessments in motor learning and/or psychological/ behavioral theory.	TC demonstrates knowledge of the various theories and applies the theories to teaching. Practice conditions allow for individual differences. TC controls student behavior through the use of proactive strategies (i.e., catch them when they are good, awarding positive behavior, etc.). TC meets the criterion score established by the program on assessments in motor learning and psychological/ behavioral theory.	TC applies motor learning, psychological and behavioral theory appropriately in planning for and delivering instruction. Practice conditions allow for individual differences, and practice conditions are adjusted based on student responses. TC controls student behavior using proactive strategies, including encouraging student self-responsibility. TC exceeds the criterion score established by the program on assessments in motor learning and psychological/ behavioral theory.

Continued

Element	Unacceptable	Acceptable	Target
1.3 Describe and apply motor development theory and principles related to skillful movement, physical activity and fitness.	TC applies motor development theory and principles in planning for the lesson, but fails to account for developmental differences during instruction and practice activities. TC fails to meet the criterion score established by the program on assessments in motor development.	TC applies motor development theory and principles appropriately in planning for and delivering instruction. TC plans and implements lessons that are developmentally appropriate (neither too hard nor too easy). TC demonstrates application of motor development theory by using developmentally appropriate teaching cues and planning developmentally appropriate practice opportunities. TC meets the criterion score established by the program on assessments in motor development.	TC applies motor development theory and principles appropriately in planning for and delivering instruction (for all stages of student proficiency); evidence is provided by K-12 students' changes in behavior (learning occurs) in skillful movements, physical activities and personal fitness. TC exceeds the criterion score established by the program on assessments of motor development.

Element	Unacceptable	Acceptable	Target
1.4 Identify historical, philosophical and social perspectives of physical education issues and legislation.	TC fails to meet criterion scores established by the program on assessments in historical, philosophical and social perspectives. Evidence could include projects, assignments, departmental examinations or state or national licensure tests.	TC meets criterion scores established by the program on assessments in historical, philosophical and social perspectives. Evidence could include projects, assignments, departmental examinations or state or national licensure tests.	TC exceeds criterion scores established by the program on assessments in historical, philosophical and social perspectives. Evidence could include projects, assignments, departmental examinations or state or national licensure tests.

Element	Unacceptable	Acceptable	Target
1.5 Analyze and correct critical elements of motor skills and performance concepts.	TC can analyze, detect and correct critical elements for all fundamental movement skills for at least one stage of proficiency in either a verbal or written format. TC can identify key elements of motor skills, but feedback on the skills is non-specific. Lessons focus on skills without consideration for the context in which skills are executed. TC provides limited feedback to students on the effective use of tactics and strategies.	TC analyzes, detects and corrects elements of all fundamental movement skills using skill cues linked to the identified critical elements. TC provides specific, corrective feedback on critical elements for motor skills. Lessons focus on skills with consideration for the context in which skills are executed. TC identifies objectives related to decision making and the use of strategies and tactics. TC provides feedback to students on the effective use of strategies and tactics.	TC analyzes, detects and corrects all students' fundamental movement skills using skill cues linked to the identified critical elements. TC provides specific, corrective feedback on critical elements for both motor skills and tactics. TC identifies objectives related to decision making and the effective use of strategies and tactics, and plans practice activities congruent to objectives. TC provides specific, corrective feedback to students on the effective use of strategies and tactics.

Standard 2: Skill-Based and Fitness-Based Competence

Physical education teacher candidates (TC) are physically educated individuals with the knowledge and skills necessary to demonstrate competent movement performance and health-enhancing fitness as delineated in the NASPE K-12 Standards.

Element	Unacceptable	Acceptable	Target
2.1 Demonstrate personal competence* in motor skill performance for a variety of physical activities and movement patterns. TC competence will be defined by the program and assessed accordingly. All programs will ensure that teacher candidates with documented disabilities are allowed and encouraged to use a variety of accommodations and/or modifications to demonstrate competency in movement fundamentals, performance concepts and fitness based on their ability.*	TC can demonstrate all fundamental movement skills at the automatic stage, but only in isolation (a non-authentic environment; not within a variety of physical activities or in coordination with other movement patterns). TC demonstrates movement skills at the control level. Skill competency is at the recreational level of motor performance.	TC demonstrates all fundamental movement patterns at the automatic stage in an authentic environment. TC demonstrates the ability to combine movement patterns into a sequence. TC demonstrates movement skills at the utilization level across a variety of physical activities. TC demonstrates competency in a variety physical activities.	TC demonstrates all fundamental movement patterns at the automatic stage in an authentic environment. TC demonstrates the ability to combine and adapt skills during game play. TC consistently performs at the utilization level of motor competency across all activities. TC demonstrates proficiency in a variety of physical activities.

Element	Unacceptable	Acceptable	Target
2.2 Achieve and maintain a health-enhancing level of fitness throughout the program. TC competence will be defined by the program and assessed accordingly. All programs will ensure that teacher candidates with documented disabilities are allowed and encouraged to use a variety of accommodations and/or modifications to demonstrate competency in movement fundamentals, performance concepts and fitness based on their ability.*	TC performs below the age- and gender-specific levels for one or more of the 5 components of health-related physical fitness (cardiorespiratory endurance, muscular strength, muscular endurance, flexibility and body composition), using standards established by national, state or program-level testing.	TC meets the age- and gender-specific levels for each of the 5 components of health-related physical fitness (cardiorespiratory endurance, muscular strength, muscular endurance, flexibility and body composition), using standards established by national, state or program-level testing.	TC exceeds the age- and gender-specific levels for each of the 5 components of health-related physical fitness (cardiorespiratory endurance, muscular strength, muscular endurance, flexibility and body composition), using standards established by national, state or program-level testing.

Continued

Element	Unacceptable	Acceptable	Target
2.3 Demonstrate performance concepts related to skillful movement in a variety of physical activities. TC competence will be defined by the program and assessed accordingly. All programs will ensure that teacher candidates with documented disabilities are allowed and encouraged to use a variety of accommodations and/or modifications to demonstrate competency in movement fundamentals, performance concepts and fitness based on their ability.*	TC cannot select what to do and/or cannot execute that selection appropriately in the authentic environment for a variety of physical activities. TC uses ineffective strategies in attempting to create open space (offensive tactics) or close open space (defensive tactics) while participating in physical activity.	TC correctly selects what to do and executes that selection appropriately in the authentic environment for a variety of physical activities. TC can apply strategies that effectively create open space (offensive tactics) and close open space (defensive tactics) while participating in physical activity.	TC correctly selects what to do and executes that selection appropriately in a variety of activities. TC executes advanced strategies using skills at appropriate times and/or appropriate situations. In addition, TC anticipates and gains an advantage while participating in physical activity.

Standard 3: Planning and Implementation

Physical education teacher candidates (TC) plan and implement developmentally appropriate learning experiences aligned with local, state and national standards to address the diverse needs of all students.

Element	Unacceptable	Acceptable	Target
3.1 Design and implement short- and long-term plans that are linked to program and instructional goals, as well as a variety of student needs.	TC fails to make both long- and short-term plans. Planning is limited to daily lesson plans, with no plan for long-term instructional goals for the unit. Lesson objectives are not aligned with identified long-term goals (unit). Planned learning activities are out of alignment with instructional or programmatic goals.	TC designs and implements short- and long-term plans. Learning activities are congruent with short-term (lesson objectives) and long-term (unit objectives) goals and are linked directly to student needs. TC uses strategies such as backward mapping in planning short- and long-term goals.	TC designs and implements short- and long-term plans, using such strategies as backward mapping to ensure that learning is sequential. Short- and long-term goals are linked directly to student learning activities. Short- and long-term goals inform instruction and learning activities and allow for differentiated instruction and multiple means of teaching sequences.

Element	Unacceptable	Acceptable	Target
3.2 Develop and implement appropriate (e.g., measurable, developmentally appropriate, performance-based) goals and objectives aligned with local, state and/or national standards.	Objectives are inappropriate for the subject area/developmental level of learners by being either too difficult or too easy. Objectives address only performance. Objectives are appropriate, but TC fails to align objectives with local, state and/or national standards.	Objectives are appropriate for subject area/developmental level of learners, are connected appropriately to the standards and provide appropriate challenges for students (tasks are neither too easy nor too difficult). Objectives are measurable, and most objectives identify criteria.	Objectives are appropriate for the subject area/developmental level of learners, are connected explicitly to the standards and provide appropriate challenges for students (tasks are neither too easy nor too difficult). Objectives incorporate multiple domains of learning or content areas. Objectives are measurable, and each contains criteria for student mastery.

Element	Unacceptable	Acceptable	Target
3.3 Design and implement content that is aligned with lesson objectives.	TC selects model/approach that is incongruent with the subject matter/content, student population and/or goals/objectives. Teaching approach does not consider the developmental level of students, context of the class (number of students in class, equipment, space, etc.), and/or the context (open or closed environment) in which the skill/activity will be performed. Students participating in the learning activities fail to achieve the lesson objectives.	TC selects teaching approach/model based on developmental level of students, context of the class and the context in which the skill/activity will be performed. Teaching approach is congruent with the goals/objectives, the number of students in the class, pre-assessment of students' developmental levels, available equipment, space and context (open or closed environment) in which the skill/activity will be performed. Learning activities allow students to achieve objectives.	TC selects teaching approach/model that is congruent with the goals/objectives and facilitates mastery. The approach/model selected maximizes practice opportunities, allows for individual differences in skill levels, maximizes the use of space and equipment, and allows students to practice tasks in appropriate environments related to the context (open or closed environment) in which the skill/activity is performed. Learning activities allow students to achieve objectives.

Continued

Element	Unacceptable	Acceptable	Target
3.4 Plan for and manage resources to provide active, fair and equitable learning experiences.	No plan (or TC does not plan or plans minimally for adaptations based on individual differences (abilities/needs/ interests). Instruction is not individualized and a "one size fits all" approach is taken. TC uses one instructional model/approach throughout the lesson. TC does not make adaptations or offer choices in equipment, space use or practice tasks based on individual differences.	TC plans for instructional adaptations for individual differences (abilities/needs/ interest). TC can articulate an appropriate rationale for adaptations. TC uses multiple instructional models/ approaches throughout the lesson to account for variations in learning styles and prior experiences. TC provides student choices in equipment, space or level of practice tasks based on individual differences.	TC's plans routinely reflect sophisticated adaptations for abilities (all levels) and needs (interests and motivation) with a sound rationale. TC uses multiple instructional models/ approaches throughout the lesson to account for variations in learning styles and prior experiences. Students are given multiple choices (equipment, space, etc.) within practice tasks, based on individual differences.
Element	Unacceptable	Acceptable	Target
3.5 Plan and adapt instruction for diverse student needs, adding specific accommodations and/or modifications for student exceptionalities.	TC fails to account for student exceptionalities or differences within the class based on factors such as gender, class, ethnicity, race, physical or mental disability, or socioeconomic status. TC does not make accommodations for the diversity found within the student population. Failure to account for exceptionalities would include such components as the choices of units to be taught, selection of students chosen to demonstrate, degree of inclusion reflected in bulletin boards or other displays and grouping of students for instruction or play. TC fails to collaborate with the IEP team on the planning and implementing of lessons that meet the needs of students with disabilities.	TC accounts for student exceptionalities or differences within the class by planning and implementing lessons that make modifications based on factors such as gender, class, ethnicity, race, physical or mental disability, or socioeconomic status. TC demonstrates teaching behaviors that reflect thoughtful consideration of exceptionalities through such behaviors as the selection of units to be taught, inclusion of diversity in bulletin boards and other displayed materials, using a variety of students to demonstrate and grouping students for instruction and play. TC collaborates with the IEP team on the implementation of lessons that meet the needs of students with disabilities.	TC accounts for exceptionalities among students or makes accommodations for the diversity found within the student population using creativity and foresight. It is clear from TC behaviors that components such as selection of units of instruction, materials selected for display, selection of students to demonstrate and methods of grouping students that exceptionalities and diversity found within the student population and have driven instructional decision-making. TC collaborates with the IEP team on the planning and implementing of lessons that meet the needs of students with disabilities.

Continued

Element	Unacceptable	Acceptable	Target
3.6 Plan and implement progressive, sequential instruction that addresses the diverse needs of students.	Learning tasks are inappropriate for the developmental levels of students by being either too difficult or too easy. TC fails to make adjustments to tasks to accommodate students' developmental levels by increasing or decreasing task complexity. The sequence of the lesson may be illogical, with gaps in progressions. Learning/practice tasks are arranged randomly in the lesson, with steps between progressions either too large or too small to facilitate skill mastery. TC fails to pre-assess students to determine an appropriate starting point. Students are grouped for convenience (by gender, age, etc.) without consideration of the objectives for the lesson.	TC considers the context of the teaching environment and that the context is reflected in the planning and implementation of lessons. Multiple methods are used to convey content. TC groups students in a variety of ways based on objectives for lessons. All students are expected to learn and achieve mastery. Learning tasks are appropriate for the developmental levels of students by providing appropriate challenges for students (tasks are neither too easy nor too difficult for students). TC makes some adjustments to tasks to accommodate students' developmental levels, but adjustments are across the entire class and not individualized. Progressions are sequential and progressive, with no gaps. Task complexity is appropriate for skill and developmental levels of students. The sequence of the lesson(s) is logical, with few gaps in progressions. Learning/ practice tasks are arranged in sequential and progressive steps to facilitate learning. TC pre-assesses students to determine an appropriate starting point.	Learning objectives and tasks are appropriate for the developmental level of students, providing appropriate challenges for students (tasks are neither too easy nor too difficult). TC makes adjustments to tasks based on student performance (increasing or decreasing task complexity). Adjustments are both across the entire class and individualized. The sequence of the lesson is logical with no gaps in progressions. Learning/ practice tasks allow students to begin and end at different levels based on individual readiness. Progressions are sequential, with opportunities for students to extend tasks to increase or decrease the challenge. TC individualizes starting points for students based on student pre-assessment. TC sets high expectations for all students.
Element	Unacceptable	Acceptable	Target
3.7 Demonstrate knowledge of current technology by planning and implementing learning experiences that require students to use technology appropriately to meet lesson objectives.	TC does not make appropriate use of the available technology. TC demonstrates limited knowledge of current technology and its applications in a physical activity setting. TC's use of technology does not align with lesson objectives.	TC integrates learning experiences that involve students in the use of available technology. TC demonstrates knowledge and use of current technology and applies this knowledge in the development and implementation of lessons in a physical activity setting. TC's use of technology is aligned with lesson objectives.	TC integrates learning experiences that require students to use various technologies in a physical activity setting. TC demonstrates mastery of current technologies and uses the technology to enhance student learning. TC incorporates technology such as pedometers, video, etc., to provide feedback to students. TC's use of technology is aligned with lesson objectives.

Standard 4: Instructional Delivery and Management

Physical education teacher candidates (TC) use effective communication and pedagogical skills and strategies to enhance student engagement and learning.

Element	Unacceptable	Acceptable	Target
4.1 Demonstrate effective verbal and non-verbal communication skills across a variety of instructional formats.	TC's verbal interactions have an occasional mistake in grammar, poor diction and/or inappropriate language for the age and skill level of students. The pacing of verbal communication is consistently either too fast or too slow, and there is little variation in tone and inflection. All communication is verbal, with no other form of communication used.	TC's verbal interactions have an occasional mistake in grammar or the occasional use of an inappropriate or regional colloquialism. Pacing of verbal communication is neither too fast nor too slow, with some variation in tone and inflection. Verbal and non-verbal communication is used throughout the lesson. TC uses alternative forms of communication, such as task sheets, bulletin boards, etc., to communicate content.	TC uses proper grammar and diction. Pacing of verbal communication is appropriate for age group (neither too fast nor too slow) and is varied in tone and inflection. Multiple forms of communication, such as task sheets, bulletin boards, etc., are used throughout the lesson.

Element	Unacceptable	Acceptable	Target
4.2 Implement effective demonstrations, explanations and instructional cues and prompts to link physical activity concepts to appropriate learning experiences.	TC either provides no demonstration or an incorrect demonstration during the instructional episode. TC provides either too few or too many instructional cues or prompts for the developmental level of students. Instructional cues are incorrect or do not identify key elements of the skill/strategies.	TC provides an effective demonstration/model during the instructional episode. TC creates instructional cues or prompts that identify key elements of the skill/strategies and are appropriate for the developmental level of students. TC repeats the cues/prompts multiple times during the lesson.	TC provides an effective demonstration/model during the instructional episode. TC creates innovative instructional cues/prompts to facilitate learning including such things as rhymes or finding ways to make abstract concepts concrete. TC consistently repeats the instructional cues or prompts throughout the lesson.

Element	Unacceptable	Acceptable	Target
4.3 Provide effective instructional feedback for skill acquisition, student learning and motivation.	TC provides generalized feedback without connecting the feedback to a specific response. Feedback is motivational and not corrective. Feedback is provided to the group as a whole.	TC provides both generalized and corrective feedback that is well-timed. Feedback is linked directly to student responses. A combination of positive, specific and corrective feedback is used. Both individual and group feedback is given.	TC provides positive, specific, corrective feedback that is well-timed. Feedback is linked directly to student responses and identifies key elements. Both individual and group feedback is given.

Element	Unacceptable	Acceptable	Target
4.4 Recognize the changing dynamics of the environment and adjust instructional tasks based on student responses.	TC delivers lessons by remaining on script without regard to student responses. TC fails to recognize changes in the teaching environment or fails to make adjustments based on changes in the environment.	TC makes adjustments to planned lessons based on student responses. TC demonstrates flexibility in the lesson or with students by adjusting lessons based on student responses.	TC demonstrates flexibility and creativity when adjusting the lesson based on student responses. TC responds appropriately to teachable moments during the lesson.

Continued

Element	Unacceptable	Acceptable	Target
4.5 Use managerial rules, routines and transitions to create and maintain a safe and effective learning environment.	TC uses ineffective rules or has difficulty in implementing classroom rules. Rules lack clarity or are stated in language inappropriate for the age group. Managerial routines are not present, and no systems are in place for distribution/return of equipment, attendance, finding a partner or creating a group, and other gymnasium routines. Arrangement of students does not allow them to practice tasks. Spacing for tasks impedes student practice (too close or too far apart). There is not a clear stop and start signal in place. Behavior issues are addressed insufficiently or ineffectively.	TC has established rules for the classroom and enforces these rules consistently. Rules are stated in developmentally appropriate language. Managerial routines are present and a system is in place for distribution/return of equipment, attendance, finding a partner or creating a group, and other gymnasium routines. There is a clear stop and start signal in place. Effective use of space is evident in the lesson (students are neither too far apart nor too close together). Behavior issues are addressed immediately, efficiently and effectively by such proactive strategies as student prompts. TC creates a supportive environment that invites student participation.	TC has established rules that are logical, reasonable and developmentally appropriate, with clear consequences for discipline issues. Rules are enforced consistently. Managerial routines are present and innovative, such as multiple equipment-distribution points. Stop and start signals are clear and creative. Space use is maximized through careful planning, with students participating in the organization of the space for their use. Students consistently self-manage their behavior during lessons. TC creates an environment in which students are encouraged and supported.
Element	Unacceptable	Acceptable	Target
4.6 Implement strategies to help students demonstrate responsible personal and social behaviors in a productive learning environment.	TC relies on direct instruction for each lesson. Students are not allowed to make decisions in the context of the class. Students' only choice is to participate or not to participate in the lesson.	TC selects both direct and indirect instructional approaches, including task and inquiry (problem solving). Students are given choices throughout the lesson about equipment, starting points or partners or groups.	TC selects both direct and indirect instructional approaches, including cooperative learning, peer teaching and student-designed instruction. Students are given multiple choices during the lesson.

Standard 5: Impact on Student Learning
Physical education teacher candidates (TC) use assessments and reflection to foster student learning and inform decisions about instruction.

Element	Unacceptable	Acceptable	Target
5.1 Select or create appropriate assessments that will measure student achievement of the goals and objectives.	TC shows no (or minimal) evidence of planning for formal or informal assessment. There is no plan for record-keeping or data analysis. Assessments don't match/ measure the lesson objectives and/or standards. Some of the objectives are not assessed.	TC uses appropriate strategies to assess student learning (paper-and-pencil tests, observational checklists, etc.) regularly. TC has a plan for record-keeping and data analysis. Planned assessments are appropriate for the lesson and/or standards. Student progress is recorded.	TC uses a variety of assessments to determine that students are achieving the goals and objectives. TC assessment record-keeping allows for detailed analysis of data. Assessments are aligned directly with the goals and objectives. Some objectives/ goals are assessed using more than one assessment.
Element	**Unacceptable**	**Acceptable**	**Target**
5.2 Use appropriate assessments to evaluate student learning before, during and after instruction.	TC demonstrates no (or minimal) evidence of planning for formal or informal assessment. If assessment is used, it occurs only after instruction. Assessments do not match the lesson objectives and/ or standards. Learning/ practice opportunities are not based on pre-assessments. Instruction is informed by instructional plan, with no regard for pre-assessments or formative assessments. Grades are determined by "effort" or "participation."	TC uses formal and informal assessments. Assessments are ongoing. Learning/ practice opportunities are based on pre- and formative assessments. Assessments are used to inform instruction and to modify instruction plan. Assessment records are kept, and assessments are used to partially determine grades.	TC uses multiple assessments. Ongoing assessments as well as summative and formative assessments are used in many contexts. Record keeping provides detailed information on students and can be transformed into a format that is accessible to others (e.g., parents/ administrators). Assessments are used to inform instruction, provide feedback, communicate progress and determine grades. Learning/practice opportunities are based on pre-assessments. Formative assessments are used that allow students to achieve mastery on summative assessments.
Element	**Unacceptable**	**Acceptable**	**Target**
5.3 Use the reflective cycle to implement change in teacher performance, student learning and/or instructional goals and decisions.	TC plans lessons without considering previous accomplishments. TC plans lessons according to teaching preferences versus student needs. Learning/practice opportunities are not based on pre-assessments and students' developmental levels.	TC uses a reflective cycle (description of teaching, justification of teaching, performance, critique of teaching, setting of goals) to modify instruction, change teacher performance or implement change based on reflection. Changes based on reflection are placed into action in lessons.	TC uses a reflective cycle (description of teaching, justification of teaching, performance, critique of teaching, setting of goals) to modify instruction, change teacher performance and implement change based on reflection. Changes based on reflection are placed into action in lessons. Short- and long-term goals are modified based on the reflective cycle.

Standard 6: Professionalism

Physical education teacher candidates (TC) demonstrate dispositions that are essential to becoming effective professionals.

Element	Unacceptable	Acceptable	Target
6.1 Demonstrate behaviors that are consistent with the belief that all students can become physically educated individuals.	TC demonstrates characteristics of "motor elitism" by providing more feedback to highly skilled students. TC excludes students during the lesson by having them participate less often in drills, games or physical activity. TC fails to make adaptations in lesson for underperforming students.	TC provides equal amounts of feedback to students regardless of skill level. All students are encouraged to participate, and equitable opportunities for participation in drills, games or physical activity are provided. TC makes adaptations in lessons for underperforming students.	TC provides equal amounts of feedback to students regardless of skill level. All students are encouraged to participate, and equitable opportunities for participation in drills, games or physical activity are provided. TC makes adaptations in lesson for underperforming students. TC sets high expectations for all students.

Element	Unacceptable	Acceptable	Target
6.2 Participate in activities that enhance collaboration and lead to professional growth and development.	TC participates in professional growth and development opportunities when directed to do so. TC meets only the minimum professional-development requirements for the program. TC fails to document any collaboration with faculty, parents, supervising teachers and/or service projects, as required by the program.	TC participates in professional growth and development opportunities when they are offered. TC participates in professional opportunities beyond the program requirements, such as major's club, and attendance at state conventions, health fairs and Jump/Hoop for Hearts activities. TC documents collaboration with faculty, parents, supervising teachers and/or service projects, as required by the program.	TC takes every opportunity to participate in professional-development opportunities. TC participates in professional opportunities beyond the program requirements, such as making presentations at professional conventions, providing leadership in student groups and planning activities. TC documents collaboration with faculty, parents, supervising teachers and/or service projects beyond program requirements.

Element	Unacceptable	Acceptable	Target
6.3 Demonstrate behaviors that are consistent with the professional ethics of highly qualified teachers.	TC dresses inappropriately for school setting, in violation of school and university dress codes. TC fails to maintain confidentiality regarding colleagues, students or families. TC demonstrates favoritism for specific students or groups of students. TC has inappropriate contact with students outside of the classroom or uses inappropriate language with or around students. TC exhibits behaviors that are indicative of gender or racial bias.	TC's dress is consistent with school and university guidelines. TC maintains confidentiality regarding colleagues, students and families. TC demonstrates behaviors that are consistent with equitable treatment for all students. TC maintains professional relationships with students in and out of the school setting.	TC's dress exceeds the requirements of the school and university guidelines. TC maintains confidentiality regarding colleagues, students and families. TC demonstrates behaviors that are consistent with equitable treatment for all students and that foster an environment in which all students are respectful of one another. TC maintains professional relationships with students in and out of the school setting.

Continued

Element	Unacceptable	Acceptable	Target
6.4 Communicate in ways that convey respect and sensitivity.	TC interacts with others in a professional manner, but sometimes resorts to the use of "slang" terms during conversations with students. TC sometimes "puts down" students in front of classmates. TC occasionally demonstrates behaviors or language that is insensitive to cultural differences.	TC attempts to teach in a culturally responsive way. TC demonstrates respect for cultural differences and exhibits teaching behaviors that are inclusive. TC avoids sarcasm and "put downs" while interacting with students.	TC teaches using culturally responsive approaches. TC demonstrates respect for cultural differences and creates an atmosphere in the classroom that is inclusive. TC never uses "put downs" or sarcasm while teaching.

CHAPTER 2
Assessing the Initial Standards

This chapter addresses how faculty members can assess the extent to which teacher candidates — individually and collectively — demonstrate the knowledge, skills and dispositions described in the Initial PETE Standards.

After unpacking the standards and elements, faculty members need to ensure that the assessment criteria for candidate performance are clear, measurable and aligned with the intent of the targeted NASPE standard or element. These standards-based assessments must be administered to all candidates in the program. Finally, faculty must analyze individual and aggregated data to interpret program effectiveness relative to the standards, and then make relevant changes to improve candidate performance and program effectiveness. This chapter provides information regarding alignment, scoring guide development, assessments and how to analyze and interpret individual and aggregated data for program improvement.

Standards-Based Assessment

Standards-based assessment is a process of determining the extent to which a candidate "… can demonstrate … understanding and ability relative to identified standards of learning" (Lambert, 1999, p. 6). In other words, PETE programs can use data generated from assessments to determine candidate proficiency in relation to NASPE Standards.

When they aggregate assessment data from candidates, PETE faculty members can make inferences not only about individual candidate performance, but also about overall program effectiveness relative to the standard (NASPE, 2004). If an assessment is not aligned with a particular standard or element, the data may not be valuable in demonstrating candidate achievement related to that standard or element.

Many programs offer unique and valuable experiences that help candidates become highly qualified novice teachers. Those experiences, however, might not be aligned with NASPE's PETE standards and, therefore, would not provide evidence of meeting the standards. If a unique program experience aligns with a NASPE standard or element, and the evaluation process results in meaningful data that one can analyze and interpret, it might be worth using in a program's standards-based assessment process. However, if a unique experience *doesn't* align with a NASPE standard or element, or isn't evaluated in a manner that provides quantifiable and unbiased data, one should modify the assessment or consider a different one.

Developing Assessments

This section provides information for developing assessments that align with NASPE's PETE Standards and Elements. Programs are encouraged to implement assessments that align with their program goals and mission, as well as with NASPE's Standards. Programs will find numerous examples of assignments that they can use to provide evidence for a standard or element. Programs are free to implement sections of text, or all or none of the scoring-guide criteria provided in the sample rubrics in Chapter 1 of this book. The examples and rubrics are not intended to be prescriptive in any way; they're offered simply as aids for developing assessments and scoring guides. Programs should refer to NASPE's PETE Standards often to ensure that descriptions of the assignments, scoring guides and minimal levels of acceptable candidate performance align with the intent of any one standard or element.

The PETE Standards are written to reflect the desired outcomes of initial teacher licensure and master's-degree, post-initial licensure programs in physical education. As such, most of the assessments used to meet the standards will be administered near the end of the programs. It is understood that programs will collect formative data throughout to determine candidate competence and program effectiveness. For example, early in an initial preparation program, teacher candidates learn to write objectives, develop learning activities to meet objectives and implement lessons with peers. PETE programs can analyze and interpret data — in the form of candidate scores or grades from the assignment — to determine the extent to which candidates demonstrate the understanding and ability to plan for K-12 students at this stage of the program.

While these formative data are important to understanding how candidates demonstrate planning for instruction, they don't reflect ability to both plan and implement, as is the expectation of NASPE's Initial PETE Standard 3 and the elements that are associated with it. The assessments used to document that the 2008 Standards and Elements are met should be required of *all* candidates in the program.

Aligning Assessments With the Standards

"Alignment" describes agreement or congruence among two or more concepts or objects. With regard to program report preparation and review, alignment describes the relationship between standards and assessments used as evidence for meeting the standards. In particular, alignment occurs when the concept addressed in the standard is apparent in the assessment, and to the same depth, breadth and specificity. Because each element within a standard must be met, it's important to ensure that scoring guide criteria for all assessments align with the elements rather than holistically with any one standard.

Example: An assessment states that it provides evidence for meeting Initial PETE **Element 4.2:** *Implement effective demonstrations, explanations and instructional cues and prompts to link physical activity concepts to appropriate learning experiences.* The assessment charges teacher candidates with writing a lesson plan and implementing it with middle school students. The assignment states that teacher candidates must include a demonstration, explanation and instructional cues and prompts in the lesson plan. The scoring guide includes one item that exclusively evaluates teacher candidates' ability to plan for effective demonstrations, explanations and instructional cues and prompts. The same scoring guide also includes a second item to exclusively evaluate teacher candidates' ability to effectively implement the planned demonstrations, explanations, instructional cues and prompts with middle school students. If the term "effective" is defined using clear and distinct criteria in the scoring guide, consistent with best practice in education, this assessment can be considered to be aligned with Element 4.2.

A second example addresses Initial PETE **Element 1.5:** *Analyze and correct critical elements of motor skills and performance concepts.* Specifically, the assessment provides partial data that support teacher candidates' ability to analyze a peer's floor hockey performance when passing a puck to a teammate. This can be an important learning experience for teacher candidates, because it provides practice for what they must do as in-service physical educators. The assessment, as described here, however, doesn't align with the depth and breadth of Element 1.5. If the data are to potentially offer evidence of performance for Element 1.5, the assessment also must require teacher candidates to correct the critical elements they observe during the analysis.

In some cases, a program might be required to use an assessment that is common to other teacher education programs within the institution. These generic assessments often lack clear alignment with the PETE Standards. While many generic assessments provide some level of information regarding candidate performance in a teaching environment, they might not offer evidence of ability to plan, teach, manage and assess in a physical education environment.

To ensure that data reflect candidate ability in the physical education environment, program faculty might consider modifying generic assessments to address NASPE's PETE Standards. Modifications might include creating an addendum or including additional items that reference NASPE Standards and Elements directly. Another strategy might be to modify the scoring guide so that it addresses the alignment with the PETE Standards specifically. It's important to state explicitly how each generic assessment item aligns directly with the NASPE element the evidence is intended to support.

Developing Scoring Guides

The first step in developing a scoring guide for a specific assignment is to align all items on the guide with requirements identified in the assignment's description. Assuming that the assignment/assessment aligns with key components of the standard or element, the scoring guide then will assess those key components. It's important to follow a few simple guidelines to ensure that the scoring guide assesses key components of the assignment. The scoring guide should:

1. Identify the candidate's "observable" behaviors in the language of "actions" that the candidate takes.

2. Provide detailed feedback to the candidate on expectations for meeting the criteria set forth in the assignment.

3. Identify distinct and meaningful levels of candidate performance, going beyond a checklist or simple "yes" or "no."

4. Provide data that shows whether all candidates in the program have met the standard or element. This data analysis is critical for program improvement and to determine the program's effectiveness in preparing candidates to meet the National Standards.

"Observable" behaviors are those behaviors that others can evaluate. For example, we can't see "teaching effectiveness," but we can infer teaching effectiveness by observing candidates give " ...specific, corrective feedback to individuals and to the group" or by observing candidates as they "demonstrate skill cues from multiple angles." These teaching behaviors are observable and, therefore, can be identified in a scoring guide. Scoring guides must use language that reflects candidates' actions.

The same guidelines apply to written assignments. If the assignment requires candidates to "create developmentally appropriate learning activities," the scoring guide delineates the "observable" or "identifiable" components of a "developmentally appropriate learning activity." For example, the scoring guide might state: "The learning activities were neither too difficult nor too easy for students," or "equipment choices were aligned with students' age and developmental levels." A scoring guide that is aligned with the assignment and identifies candidates' specific observable "actions" will allow observers to determine the quality of the instruction and whether the candidates meet the standard.

Once the observable behavior is identified, the scoring guide should provide detailed feedback to candidates regarding their meeting the criteria as defined by the assignment. At a minimum, this requires a scoring guide to identify the behaviors that the candidate must manifest — and that the observers must observe — to document that the candidate has met the assignment's key component at the minimally acceptable level. For example, if the assignment requires candidates to "use appropriate assessments to evaluate student learning before, during and after instruction," the scoring guide must define those behaviors that the candidates must exhibit to ensure that they're meeting the criteria. The scoring guide might state:

> Teacher candidate uses appropriate strategies to assess student learning (paper-and-pencil test, observational checklists, etc.) regularly. Planned assessments are appropriate for lesson. Record-keeping provides information about student learning. Assessment occurs throughout the unit of instruction and is used to inform instruction, provide feedback, communicate progress and/or determine grades.

The scoring guide must align with the item on the assignment and must assess the quality of candidate performance, not simply how often a behavior occurs (i.e., "never," "sometimes," "frequently").

Some scoring guides also will identify distinct levels of candidate proficiency for each component of the assignment, which usually involves developing an analytical rubric. An analytical rubric will identify those behaviors that are below the criteria and those that are beyond the minimum criteria. Analytical rubrics typically use three to five levels. If an analytical rubric was used for the item above, the "unacceptable" level might state:

> TC demonstrates no evidence of planning for formal or informal assessment. If assessment is used, it occurs only after instruction. Learning/practice opportunities are not based on pre-assessments. Instruction is informed by instructional plan with no regard to pre-assessments or formative assessments. Grades are determined by effort or participation.

If the candidate performed beyond the minimum level, the scoring guide might state:

> TC uses multiple assessments. TC uses ongoing assessments, as well as summative and formative assessments. Record-keeping provides detailed information on students and can be transformed into a format that is accessible to others. Assessments are used to inform instruction, provide feedback, communicate progress and/or determine grades.

An analytical rubric provides candidates with specific feedback on their performance, as well as on how their performance relates to the criteria identified on the assignment. Some state and national accreditation requirements mandate that scoring guides identify distinct levels of candidate performance. (See Appendix B for a sample description of assignment and scoring guide.)

Scoring guides also must provide programs with the data they need to make informed decisions about changes or adjustments to the assignment/assessment. Therefore, data collection should be built into any scoring guide. A high-quality scoring guide allows the program to collect data about individual items, subgroups/domains of similar items or a holistic assessment of candidates' performance on the assignment. The scoring guide should allow programs to disaggregate the data by individuals, programs, gender, transfer, etc., so the program can "drill down" into the data for insight on candidate and program performance.

Using the Data for Candidate and Program Improvement

Data collected from assessments can provide candidate feedback and contribute to program improvement. Initially, program faculty members can use the assessment, scoring guide and other data to clarify expectations for candidates and to help them improve their performance as practitioners. Later, when the data have been collected and aggregated by class or year, they can provide evidence to justify changes at the program level.

Program faculty members should review these aggregated data regularly and systematically, as a means for informing discussions and decisions regarding program improvement. For example, data showing that candidates are performing at high levels can indicate program strengths. Conversely, data showing that many candidates are performing below an acceptable level can point to areas that require improvement. NASPE's 2008 Initial PETE Standards also provide PETE programs with an opportunity to audit curriculum and program requirements. as well as to ensure best practice in teacher education broadly and physical education specifically. These standards also can serve as guidelines for establishing the scope and sequence of program expectations and curriculum delivery.

EXAMPLES OF ASSESSMENTS FOR USE
WITH NASPE'S 2008 STANDARDS FOR INITIAL PETE

Standard 1: Scientific and Theoretical Knowledge
Physical education teacher candidates know and apply discipline-specific scientific and theoretical concepts critical to the development of physically educated individuals.

Examples of assessments include, but are not limited to, the following:

1. State licensure test (demonstrating candidate content knowledge of physical education).

2. Praxis II® Subject Tests for Physical Education.

3. Comprehensive institutional or program tests (demonstrating candidates' content knowledge of physical education).

4. Examination grades from selected courses (demonstrating candidates' content knowledge of physical education).

5. Course grades. (See Note 3 on p. 29.)

6. Internship assessment (as applicable for demonstrating candidates' content knowledge of physical education).

7. Movement analysis project.

8. Lesson plan.

9. Case study.

10. Portfolio. (See Note 1 on p. 29.)

11. Class project or assignment. (See Note 2 on p. 29.)

This list is not exhaustive. In most cases, one assessment might not provide enough evidence for all elements or the intent of the standard. For example, using a movement analysis project might offer evidence for meeting Element 1.5, but it might not address any of the content knowledge inherent in Element 1.4.

Another example: using a pencil-and-paper state licensure test that requires candidates to select the best response to a question related to physical education content knowledge. While this test might provide evidence for meeting the "know" portion of Standard 1, it might not provide evidence of candidates' ability to apply discipline-specific concepts.

Standard 2: Skill-Based and Fitness-Based Competence*
Physical education teacher candidates are physically educated individuals with the knowledge and skills necessary to demonstrate competent movement performance and health-enhancing fitness as delineated in the NASPE K–12 Standards.

Examples of assessments include, but are not limited to, the following:

1. Test of Gross Motor Development (TGMD-2).

2. Battery of skill and performance tests.

3. Course grades. (See Note 3 on p. 29.)

4. Scores from specific motor or fitness tests. (*Programs must set benchmark scores and identify distinct levels of competency.)

5. Comprehensive program tests (demonstrating candidates' personal competence in motor skill performance for a variety of physical activities and movement patterns).

6. A health-related fitness test (e.g., Fitnessgram**).

7. Comprehensive program tests (demonstrating candidate achievement and maintenance of a health-enhancing level of fitness throughout the program).

8. Videotape analysis of game play.

9. Assessment of candidates' analysis of performance created from a storyboard using performance analysis software.

**Programs must plan for accommodations and/or modifications for teacher candidates with documented disabilities. To avoid discrimination against those with disabilities, physical education teacher candidates with special needs are allowed and encouraged to use a variety of accommodations and/or modifications to demonstrate competent movement and performance concepts (modified/adapted equipment, augmented communication devices, multimedia devices, etc.) and fitness (weight-training programs, exercise logs, etc.).

Standard 3: Planning and Implementation
Physical education teacher candidates plan and implement developmentally appropriate learning experiences aligned with local, state and national standards to address the diverse needs of all students.

Examples of assessments include, but are not limited to, the following:

1. Unit plan.

2. Teacher work sample.

3. Portfolio. (See Note 1 on p. 29.)

4. Internship assessment.

5. Lesson plan.

6. Case study.

7. Assessment of a candidate-created sample IEP.

Candidates will create a plan for teaching K-12 students and use that plan to deliver instruction. Therefore, assignments administered to collect data regarding candidate performance for Standard 3 and its elements mandate that candidates both plan and teach the same lesson.

Standard 4: Instructional Delivery and Management
Physical education teacher candidates use effective communication and pedagogical skills and strategies to enhance student engagement and learning.

Examples of assessments include, but are not limited to, the following:

1. Internship assessment.

2. Teacher work sample.

3. Unit plan.

Assignments administered to collect data regarding candidate performance for Standard 4 and its elements require that candidates demonstrate instructional delivery skills during the lesson. Therefore, assessments aligned with Standard 4 and its elements will require observing candidates while teaching in a K–12 environment with students.

Standard 5: Impact on Student Learning
Physical education teacher candidates use assessments and reflection to foster student learning and inform decisions about instruction.

Examples of assessments include, but are not limited to, the following:

1. Teacher work sample.

2. Student assessment project.

3. Lesson plan.

4. Internship assessment.

5. Reflection paper of candidates' teaching performance.

6. Reflection requirement attached to lesson plan(s) implemented with K-12 students.

7. Unit plan (if aligned with Element 5.3).

Standard 6: Professionalism
Physical education teacher candidates demonstrate dispositions that are essential to becoming effective professionals.

Examples of assessments include, but are not limited to, the following:

1. Internship assessment.

2. Case study.

3. Portfolio. (See Note 1 at end of this chapter.)

4. Participation logs (as participation or evidence of attendance aligns with Element 6.2).

5. Candidate disposition assessment data.

Notes:

1. **Portfolios:** Many portfolio assignments require candidates to submit one or more artifacts of their best work for each NASPE standard. The candidate must submit the artifact along with a reflection statement of how the artifact aligns with the NASPE standard. Often, the evaluation of the portfolio assignment is based on the reflective statement, and a checklist ensures that all required artifacts were submitted. If the portfolio is evaluated in this manner, it's not likely to provide evidence for meeting NASPE Standards because the artifacts differ for each candidate and because a checklist doesn't address the work's quality, only its presence.

   As such, faculty members must determine the portfolio assignment's purpose and how the data generated from evaluating the portfolios align with one or more NASPE Standards. To make the portfolio assignment a viable assessment, it would be useful to:

   1. Require specific mandated artifacts as evidence for each standard or element related to a standard.

   2. Provide a scoring guide for how each artifact is evaluated as it aligns with the standard or element's intent.

2. **Class Project or Assignment:** The data should be culled from assignments that charge candidates with independent work rather than assignments that require them to submit work in groups of two or more. If candidates are working in pairs or groups larger than a pair, it's difficult to determine the extent to which the data represent knowledge or skills related to each candidate.

   The exception to this requirement occurs when candidates are charged to work in pairs to team-teach or implement plans with K-12 students, and the university supervisor and/or mentor teacher evaluates candidates on an *individual* basis. That should be stated explicitly on assessment documents to avoid confusion about how grading is administered.

3. **Course Grades:** If a program uses course grades as evidence of candidate content knowledge, the courses selected must be required of all candidates in the program. The only exception to this rule is when a candidate selects from an approved menu of courses required in a specific sub-content area. *Example:* An initial licensure program might permit candidates to take and pass two courses from a "team sport" menu that includes up to six course choices.

   Keep in mind that one can't determine the extent to which data from grades offer evidence of candidates' content knowledge when the assessment fails to describe adequately what the grades are intended to measure. Using course grades or GPAs is limited to Standards 1 and 2 in the Initial Standards.

CHAPTER 3

2008 National Standards for Advanced Physical Education Teacher Education

This chapter provides an introduction to the 2008 National Standards for Advanced Physical Education Teacher Education (PETE), as well as offering descriptive explanations and rubrics. Each section contributes to understanding the 2008 Advanced Standards and their use in reviewing master's degree programs in physical education teacher education.

The descriptive explanation associated with each standard provides the context and rationale for selecting the skills, knowledge and performance that are envisioned as characteristics of a knowledgeable master's degree candidate. The rubrics were developed from this supporting narrative. Thus, a thorough understanding of the explanation is necessary for understanding the rubrics' concise language.

The Advanced PETE Standards are used in the NASPE/NCATE national recognition process to review advanced-level (i.e., master's degree, post-initial licensure) programs. Institutions that offer a master's degree program designed for initial preparation and licensure or certification to teach should use NASPE's Initial PETE Standards for national recognition review. In cases in which the advanced degree is in kinesiology, curriculum and instruction or education in general, rather than in physical education pedagogy, the institution should consider carefully whether a review using these Advanced Standards is appropriate.

Guiding Principles

NASPE identified four fundamental beliefs that serve as the guiding principles for creating and organizing the Advanced Standards and for developing the rubrics that describe unacceptable, acceptable and target performance levels.

1. **Focus on Learning Rather Than Teaching.** These standards and rubrics represent a belief in an approach to teaching (and to its evaluation) that focuses on learner outcomes and experiences rather than on what the teacher does (Hargreaves & Fink, 2006; Huba & Freed, 2000; NCATE 2008). The desired result of this type of teaching in physical education is individuals who are empowered to take control of and responsibility for their own ability to create healthy, active lifestyles. Critical components that distinguish acceptable and target performance levels include the ability to differentiate instruction for individual students and to include students in making decisions about their learning in ways that are developmentally appropriate. Therefore, acceptable-level descriptors, particularly for Standards 1 and 2, represent generalized pedagogical content knowledge and effective instruction practice that accommodates individual differences. Target-level descriptors go further in recognizing and capitalizing on each individual's unique characteristics, needs and

contributions. This focus on learning applies to teachers, as well as to students, and the revised Advanced Standards clearly reflect the notion that advanced teachers are, and must be, learners themselves. As Easton (2008) notes:

> It is clearer today than ever that educators need to learn, and that's why *professional learning* has replaced *professional development*. Developing is not enough. Educators must be knowledgeable and wise. They must know enough in order to change. They must change in order to get different results. They must become learners, and they must be *self*-developing (p. 756).

Thus, these Advanced Standards don't prescribe courses and experiences for advanced teacher candidates or for their continued learning. Instead, they focus on what these candidates learn and how they apply their knowledge to enhance learning in others.

2. **Integrated Knowledge Base.** Linked closely to the outcomes-based approach is the belief that an advanced teacher must possess an integrated body of knowledge and skills. The importance of an integrated knowledge base is clearly supported by seminal works in identifying and developing teaching expertise (Berliner, 1994; Clark & Peterson, 1986). Moreover, this notion is firmly underpinned by Shulman's (2004a, 2004b) definition of pedagogical content knowledge (PCK) as the teacher's knowledge of and skill for "representing and formulating the subject that makes it comprehensible to others" (p. 203). Shulman contends further that acquiring PCK depends on two main elements:

    a. A deep and broad knowledge of content and how it is learned (Professional Knowledge).

    b. The ability to help students learn specific information through understanding why the learners find those topics difficult (Professional Practice).

This integration of content and pedagogical knowledge results in and contributes to the development, application and communication of a teacher candidate's PCK, which, in turn, advances the candidate's expertise and enhances student learning.

3. **Importance of Inquiry.** The importance and value of inquiry is another key belief imbedded in these standards and rubrics. While reflective practice is considered appropriate and adequate for initial teacher candidates, those who have completed a graduate-degree program are held to a higher standard. They are expected to examine their practice in a more systematic and formal way, reflecting the rigors of having completed a master's degree, as well as demonstrating their skills as master teachers. Shulman (2004c) writes that, if teaching excellence is truly to develop, inquiry into one's own teaching is essential for practitioners. Descriptors of acceptable performance in Standard 2 identify regular and systematic analysis of one's own practice; target performance extends inquiry to the level of testing hypotheses (through interpretive or positivist approaches) and generating new knowledge that can be shared with the professional community.

4. **Role of Leadership.** Conducting inquiry into one's own or others' practice and sharing the results leads naturally into the role of professional leader. Being a professional leader means participating in a community of scholars, and mandates that advanced teachers "not only investigate teaching" but be "teachers under investigation" (Shulman, 2004c, p. 296).

Thus, the integrated knowledge base described above also must include the skills, knowledge and dispositions to inquire about teaching (Professional Knowledge), as well as to contribute to the professional learning of others for the sake of advancing the profession (Professional Leadership) and, ultimately, benefiting students (Professional Practice).

Scope/Delimitations of the Advanced Standards

Standard 1. Professional Knowledge. The question of what constitutes the content knowledge necessary for effective teaching in physical education continues to be debated (e.g., Rink, 2007). Meeting the Initial PETE Standards ensures that candidates have a foundational knowledge of both movement and pedagogy drawn from the fields of kinesiology, education and psychology. At the advanced level, it's not enough to simply add more knowledge in these areas; it's critical that candidates find new and meaningful ways to use their existing knowledge (Rink, French, Lee, Solmon, & Lynn, 1994) and/or make new connections within existing knowledge to gain understanding of how to apply their knowledge to physical education teaching. Also, candidates must acquire knowledge and skill related to inquiry in the field, which, in turn, will help them access, analyze and integrate knowledge.

Because of the breadth of content knowledge that physical education teaching requires and the differences in philosophical approaches to physical education, the Advanced Standards prescribe no specific courses or number of content or research courses.

Standard 2. Professional Practice. These Advanced Standards are purposely written in a way that requires candidates to demonstrate their ability to integrate and apply the skills, knowledge and dispositions acquired in both their initial and advanced preparation programs rather than to demonstrate isolated techniques to meet discrete standards for each aspect of the teaching/learning process. Instead of requiring programs to teach specific techniques (such as the use of technology) or concepts (such as knowledge of specific instructional models), using and integrating such techniques and concepts appropriately to enhance student learning is what is important.

Assessing candidates' knowledge of good practice serves as evidence for Standard 1; assessing their ability to integrate and implement effective, appropriate knowledge and practices provides evidence for Standard 2.

Standard 3. Professional Leadership. Ongoing professional learning lies at the heart of becoming an advanced teacher leader. Nevertheless, the Advanced Standards and rubrics don't include expectations of membership in professional organizations or participation in professional conferences. This is not meant to minimize the value of such activities, but rather to shift the focus to the impact of such activities on practice. It also reflects the practical difficulties involved in requiring memberships or conference attendance as criteria for program review.

Because those opportunities might not be available to all candidates in advanced programs, the rubrics for this standard don't address them. Programs that do offer such opportunities to their candidates and that assess this type of engagement may include those results in their sources of evidence.

Assumptions About Candidates and Programs

These Advanced Standards assume that candidates entering graduate programs already possess the basic knowledge, skills and dispositions expected of a licensed educator. Institutions are responsible for ensuring that candidates possess initial certification or licensure in physical education before being admitted to the advanced program. Institutions that admit candidates who possess certification or licensure to teach physical education but don't possess all the skills, knowledge and dispositions reflected in the Initial PETE Standards must provide opportunities for candidates to acquire them. If not, these candidates won't have the knowledge and skill underpinnings they need to meet the Advanced Standards at the "acceptable" performance level.

Because developing advanced competencies requires opportunities to implement and apply knowledge, skills and dispositions, advanced programs are expected to provide appropriate field or clinical settings in which candidates work directly with students and other education professionals. For candidates who are employed concurrently as physical educators, their work settings will generally provide an appropriate context for developing and demonstrating advanced knowledge, skills and dispositions.

Providing opportunities to develop and demonstrate teaching skills in authentic settings is especially important for those candidates who enter advanced programs without prior teaching experience. The "wisdom of practice" doesn't necessarily come quickly. Understanding the nuances of teaching and learning usually comes as "slow knowing" (Hargreaves & Fink, 2006, p. 43) from processing experiences over time. Programs are responsible for establishing the qualifications required for admission, as well as for their content and sequence. Therefore, programs must assess applicants' potential for developing to the advanced level within the length and context of the program. This is particularly important for those who are not experienced teachers.

Relationship to Initial Standards

As NASPE crafted these Advanced Standards, it considered the composition and direction of the proposed revisions to the Initial Standards as requisite proficiencies upon which to build the Advanced Standards. Thus, these Advanced Standards represent the next step on the continuum of teacher development.

NASPE's goal in revising the Advanced Standards is to set acceptable and target performance levels from which candidates emerge as competent, confident and knowledgeable professional teacher leaders. Having acquired in their initial program the basic technical skills of teaching, coupled with solid, foundational knowledge of movement and pedagogy, master's-level candidates are challenged to:

- Form connections among deeper understandings of the knowledge bases;

- Represent and communicate content through meaningful, integrated instruction; and

- Develop a professional identity emanating from rich and varied leadership experiences.

The Advanced Standards differ from the Initial Standards in three principal ways:

1. The expectation that systematic inquiry becomes a sustained and trusted practice for evaluating and improving teaching and learning.

2. Planning, teaching and assessment become interwoven into a single, simultaneous process that results in instruction tailored to the needs of **all** learners.

3. The benefits of professional development extend beyond one's own practice for the betterment of others and the improvement of the profession as a whole.

Relationship to 2001 Advanced Standards

At first glance, the 2008 Advanced Standards appear to differ substantially from the 2001 Advanced Standards (NASPE, 2001). A closer examination, though, reveals that the differences are not so great. While NASPE has reduced the number of standards from nine to three, the rigor and expectations called for in these three standards have not lessened. Instead, NASPE has reconceptualized, rewritten and expanded the concepts within the 2001 Advanced Standards and woven them into three comprehensive and focused standards that are soundly connected.

The new Standard 1 — Professional Knowledge — encompasses (and expands upon) the previous standards of Content Knowledge, Curricular Knowledge and Methods of Inquiry. The new Standard 2 — Professional Practice — includes (and integrates) Sound Teaching Practices; Assessment; Equity, Fairness and Diversity; and Reflection. The new Standard 3 — Professional Leadership — comprises Collaboration, Reflection, Leadership and Professionalism; Mentoring; and High Expectations for a Physically Active Lifestyle.

The Advanced Standards are sequenced purposely to present a progression in which the skills and knowledge of one standard serve as the basis for the next. Professional Knowledge serves as a necessary foundation, but the importance of that content knowledge is in its application to Professional Practice. And, while individual Professional Practice is important, Professional Leadership goes a step beyond, by identifying expectations for using advanced skills, knowledge and dispositions to advance the practice of others and the profession as a whole.

Meeting the Standards

Programs must demonstrate that their candidates meet all elements, because the standards and elements are linked inextricably. Meeting a standard holistically without meeting each of its elements is not possible. Only when it meets all elements can a program be assured that its graduates are truly advanced physical education teachers.

NASPE recommends that programs use multiple sources of evidence to demonstrate achievement, and that each assessment serves as a source of evidence for more than one standard. For example, assessing a thesis, creative component or action research project might provide evidence for all three standards: applying content knowledge to practice, demonstrating the types and effectiveness of instructional strategies used in teaching and disseminating findings through presentation or publication. The onus is on the program to show how such a study serves as evidence for each standard. One source of evidence alone, however, would not be adequate to satisfy all standards and all elements.

The rubrics presented in this chapter for reviewing advanced programs identify three levels of performance: "unacceptable," "acceptable" and "target." The knowledge, skills and dispositions identified as "unacceptable" represent practice that is below what is expected of advanced candidates. "Acceptable" performance is considered the minimum level necessary to meet a standard. "Target" represents the desired performance level. Candidates must meet the element at the acceptable level to meet it at the target level. Programs should strive to ensure that candidates reach target-level performance. This might be difficult for candidates who enter advanced programs without prior teaching experience.

STANDARDS, DESCRIPTIVE EXPLANATIONS AND RUBRICS

Standard 1: Professional Knowledge
Advanced physical education teacher candidates come to understand disciplinary content knowledge, the application of content knowledge to teaching physical education, and modes of inquiry that form the bases for physical education programs and instruction.

Content Knowledge

Content knowledge in physical education teacher education derives from knowledge of movement and of pedagogy. Knowledge of movement includes mastery of movement forms (e.g., games, sports, dance, aquatics, leisure activities) and information from kinesiology-related areas (e.g., exercise physiology, biomechanics, sport psychology/sociology, motor learning). Knowledge of pedagogy derives from education (e.g., education foundations, instructional technology, general methods) and psychology (e.g., child development, cognitive psychology). Advanced physical education teachers possess breadth and depth of content knowledge (Schempp, Manross, Tan & Fincher, 1998). Research on teaching in general, and in physical education specifically, indicates that a profound content knowledge base lies at the core of good teaching (Schempp, et al., 1998) and is essential to the teacher's ability to enhance student learning (Rovegno, 1995).

Advanced teachers view physical education content as more than physically active motor play and the related knowledge about these activities. In addition to updating and expanding their knowledge of movement forms continually, advanced teachers differ from initial-level teachers in their ability to find new and meaningful ways to use their existing knowledge (Rink, et al., 1994) of movement forms to achieve student outcomes beyond just skill acquisition. Advanced teachers possess a deep understanding of the content and are able to draw upon that knowledge to enhance students' overall development (Manross & Templeton, 1997).

Even experts don't know everything about their field. Therefore, advanced teacher candidates shouldn't be expected to have deep knowledge or mastery in all aspects of movement and pedagogy, but they should be well versed in several. What's essential is that they know how to relate their content knowledge to the teaching of physical education.

Developing Pedagogical Content Knowledge

Recognizing that excellent teaching results from the nexus of content and pedagogical knowledge, accomplished physical education teachers present the content so that learners comprehend the subject matter (Shulman, 2004d; Rink, 2007; Griffin, Dodds, & Rovegno, 1996). This blending of content and pedagogical knowledge is known widely as pedagogical content knowledge, or PCK (Shulman, 2004a). PCK enables teachers to predict and identify barriers to student learning and "provide remedies to overcome student difficulties" (Schempp, et al., 1998, p. 353).

Advanced teachers also know that classrooms are filled with an increasingly diverse student population representing a variety of contexts and settings. It's not enough to design instruction to address students' general characteristics; teachers must tailor instruction to the variations in ability and background presented by the learners and the learning context (Shulman, 2004b). Thus, advanced candidates must know how to combine content and pedagogical knowledge to make physical education meaningful for **all** students.

Creating New Knowledge

Possessing content knowledge is necessary but not sufficient to ensure success, and advanced teachers know that (Dodds, 1994). These teachers seek, reflect on, analyze, synthesize, create and disseminate the best available knowledge on physical education content and pedagogy to teach and to improve their teaching practice over time (Shulman, 2004c). Knowing how to do this enables teachers to "review, renew and extend" (O'Sullivan & Deglau, 2006, p. 441) their commitment to teaching.

As lifelong learners, advanced teachers use technology or other relevant tools to locate research reports, conceptual articles, Web sites and other resources that are pertinent to their teaching and learning. They then organize, analyze and interpret the information so that they can apply their findings to their teaching.

Advanced teachers design research — formal or informal, brief or extensive, classroom-based or schoolwide — focused on meaningful aspects of teaching and learning. They apply knowledge and skills of inquiry to assessing student learning. They also use inquiry to enhance and extend their content and pedagogical knowledge, and use their understanding of diverse learners' growth and development to enhance the learning environment for all students. Knowing how to systematically formulate a research question, gather and interpret data to answer the question, and communicate the findings to appropriate audiences is essential (Shulman, 2004c). Thus, advanced candidates must to know how to use a range of research and assessment methods from both positivist and interpretive paradigms.

Standard 1: Professional Knowledge

Advanced physical education teacher candidates (AC) come to understand disciplinary content knowledge, the application of content knowledge to teaching physical education, and modes of inquiry that form the bases for physical education programs and instruction.

Element	Unacceptable	Acceptable	Target
1a. Knowledge of content in movement and pedagogy.	AC has a broad understanding of movement or pedagogy. Or, AC understands both without knowing how they relate to learning and teaching in physical education.	AC has a depth of understanding in several aspects of both movement and pedagogy and can explain how they relate to learning and teaching in physical education.	AC synthesizes concepts from multiple aspects of both movement and pedagogy and can articulate how that information applies to specific students and contexts.
Element	**Unacceptable**	**Acceptable**	**Target**
1b. Knowledge of how to represent content knowledge to make it comprehensible to learners (i.e., pedagogical content knowledge).	AC knows that the integration of content and pedagogy is central to learning and teaching in physical education.	AC knows how to transform the content into understandable forms adapted to general learner characteristics.	AC knows how to transform the content into understandable forms tailored to the variations in ability and background presented by the learners and the learning context.
Element	**Unacceptable**	**Acceptable**	**Target**
1c. Knowledge of processes and methods of systematic intentional inquiry about learning and teaching in physical education.	AC has general understanding of systematic inquiry, takes research findings at face value and tries to apply them to learning and teaching in physical education.	AC has a thorough understanding of multiple modes of inquiry and can critique, synthesize and apply research findings to learning and teaching in physical education.	AC identifies pertinent questions about learning and teaching in physical education, as well as designs processes for collecting, analyzing and interpreting data to answer those questions.

Goals of Teaching in Physical Education

The essence of teaching is facilitating and enhancing the growth and development of others. The ultimate goal is to provide learning experiences that benefit learners' psychomotor, cognitive and affective development (NASPE, 2007) and to prepare those learners for their role as active members of society. Teaching in physical education seeks to enhance student learning and development in a movement environment. The intent of instruction in physical education is two-fold:

1. To enable students to acquire movement skills and knowledge.

2. To help students develop the skills necessary to take control of their own learning and decision-making (Mosston & Ashworth, 2002).

These outcomes prepare students to achieve and maintain healthy, active lifestyles so that they are willing, able and interested in seeking a lifetime of physical activity (NASPE, 2007).

Alignment of Planning, Instruction and Assessment

Advanced teachers integrate and apply content knowledge and pedagogical content knowledge (PCK) to designing, implementing and evaluating lessons and units of instruction that are appropriate for specific students in a given context. They view planning, instruction, assessment and reflection as inseparable components of an integrated process. These components are aligned with desired goals and objectives to make learning purposeful and meaningful for students.

Advanced teachers take that approach a step further by engaging learners in the process of identifying personally relevant goals and activities in a developmentally appropriate manner. Thus, they align learning experiences with specific learner needs and preferences. In addition to planning and implementing learning experiences to achieve short-term (daily and/or unit) outcomes, advanced teachers also apply these principles to achieving long-term outcomes and goals through curriculum and program development.

Differentiation of Instruction

Advanced teachers recognize both the general progression of learning in the subject/skill area and individual variations in progress toward achieving desired outcomes. They connect learning experiences to learners' prior knowledge and experience and tailor instruction to specific learner needs (Shulman, 2004b). This attention to student diversity refers not only to students with conditions typically referred to as "disabilities," but also to other forms of diversity within the general population.

To help make those connections, advanced teachers include multiple representations of the content (which might include using instructional technologies) and a range of learning experiences within a lesson or unit to address the range of learner needs. In addition, advanced teachers encourage and empower learners to monitor their own learning and needs and to seek experiences and solutions that are relevant to them. Thus, critical thinking and problem solving become part of learner development.

Investigation of Practice

Advanced teachers go beyond informal reflection to review and analyze the effect and effectiveness of their practice, including curriculum, instructional strategies and assessment, as well as their interaction with and understanding of their students. They apply their knowledge of modes of inquiry to the conduct of systematic inquiry: formulating questions, gathering and analyzing information and using the results to improve practice (Shulman, 2004c). Advanced teachers extend this process by engaging students in inquiry.

Standard 2: Professional Practice

Advanced physical education teacher candidates (AC) use content knowledge and pedagogical content knowledge (PCK) to design and conduct appropriate learning experiences that facilitate and enhance the growth of learners.

Element	Unacceptable	Acceptable	Target
2a. Teaching reflects understanding and application of content knowledge and pedagogical content knowledge appropriate to the learners, the learning environment and long- and short-term outcomes/goals.	AC demonstrates, through planning and/or instruction, limited or shallow understanding of content knowledge and PCK appropriate for the specific learners, context and/or long- and short-term outcomes/goals. Or, AC's planning and/or instruction reveals gaps or misunderstandings in content knowledge or PCK.	AC demonstrates, through planning and/or instruction, accurate and sufficient content knowledge and PCK appropriate for the specific learners, context and long- and short-term outcomes/goals.	AC demonstrates, through planning and/or instruction, a deep understanding of content knowledge and PCK, and articulates a rationale for instructional choices. Or, AC discovers opportunities to refine or develop new understandings that add to the professional body of knowledge.
Element	**Unacceptable**	**Acceptable**	**Target**
2b. Teaching reflects integration of planning, instruction and assessment as a unified process to achieve long- and short-term outcomes/goals.	AC aligns some — but not all — of the components of the learning cycle (planning, instruction, assessment and reflection) with the other components, learner needs and/or long- and short-term outcomes/goals. Or, AC's teaching deviates from planned activities so that desired goals are not assessed or achieved.	AC uses knowledge of learners' current levels of progress in achieving desired outcomes/goals (results of prior assessment) to design and carry out appropriate sequential learning experiences and instructional activities, and to assess learner progress and/or achievement. The results of this latter assessment are then used to further design or modify and carry out future learning experiences.	AC uses learners' prior knowledge and personal history (e.g., language, culture, family and community) to plan, implement and assess meaningful learning experiences. AC engages learners in the process of defining long- and short-term outcomes/goals, designing or choosing learning experiences and monitoring their own learning in ways that are developmentally appropriate.

Continued

Element	Unacceptable	Acceptable	Target
2c. Teaching reflects differentiation of instruction based on personal and cultural characteristics of learners.	AC provides the same learning experiences for all learners regardless of their personal strengths, characteristics and/ or experience. Or, the range of learner characteristics and needs exceeds the multiple learning experiences provided.	AC uses multiple representations and explanations of concepts, a variety of appropriate learning tasks and structures and a variety of assessment strategies to design and/or adapt instruction to meet the current needs of individual learners.	AC establishes a learning environment that respects and celebrates learners' diverse experiences and approaches to learning. AC uses multiple strategies to engage learners in appropriate opportunities that promote development of performance capabilities, critical-thinking skills and/ or the ability to recognize their own needs and seek experiences to meet those needs.
Element	Unacceptable	Acceptable	Target
2d. Teaching reflects systematic inquiry about the practice and the learners served.	AC places responsibility on learners for failure to achieve desired outcomes. And/or, the reflective cycle and assessment are too shallow to provide insight about ways to improve practice.	AC regularly and systematically analyzes the effectiveness of instruction on learner engagement and progress in meeting short- and long-term goals. AC takes responsibility for using this information to modify instruction and develop professional learning goals and plans.	AC engages learners in the process of analyzing teaching effectiveness and learning, and uses the results of systematic analysis to test hypotheses and generate knowledge according to the methods of inquiry and standards of evidence used in physical education.

Leadership

Leadership in the broad sense is about renewing a culture of learning and improvement at all levels of the school's organization structure through inquiry, professional learning communities, involvement in school decision-making and professional learning networks (Hargreaves & Fink, 2006). The ultimate goal of learning among professionals is to "continuously seek, share learning and act on that learning" (Hord, 1997, p. 1) for the benefit of students.

Easton (2008) prefers the term "professional *learning*" rather than "professional *training*" or "professional *development*" to reflect how teachers must continue to learn and self-develop; or, as she says, "how teachers change the way they work as a result of their learning" (Easton, 2008, p. 758). Building a culture of learning is characterized by inquiry and reflection in an ongoing collaborative environment in which teachers learn from one another, take part in school-based conversations, think differently about leadership and governance, as well as " … about data collection and use, about appropriate learning activities, about evaluation of professional learning, about role changes and — ultimately — about cultural changes that both promote and result from learning" (Easton, 2008, p. 756).

Extending and Sharing Knowledge

Teacher-to-teacher communication about teaching and learning provides a powerful source of professional learning and instructional improvement (Sparks, 2003). Communication might begin as reflective practice that engages teachers in dialog about their craft with trusted colleagues. Advanced teachers, on the other hand, extend the reflective process to a level at which they examine assumptions and practices critically through formal inquiry (Ferraro, 2000). Inquiry becomes a process originating at the bottom, within schools, "with educators identifying what students need and so what they themselves need to learn" (Easton, 2008, p. 758). It stimulates constant questioning and seeking answers about student work, teacher practices, assessments, organization structures and content in a supportive, collegial environment that honors the contributions of school staff members, as well as those of educators.

Advanced teachers seize opportunities to grow toward greater professionalism by working with students and teachers as facilitators, mentors and/or coaches, or by collaborating with colleagues on school-improvement teams and committees (Easton, 2008; Hargreaves & Fink, 2006; Mihans, 2008). Often, these endeavors lead to initiatives such as offering advice to a new colleague, trying out a new technique with students, modeling effective professional practice or taking an action research approach to solving a real classroom issue or school problem. In this sense, one practices leadership as an activity while in the role of teacher, thereby breaking with the traditional notion that only those in formalized administrative positions express leadership (Spillane, 2006).

Ongoing Development

The goal of practicing leadership that puts student learning at the core of teaching becomes possible when teachers, parents, communities and administrators participate together in cultivating an environment of sustainable school leadership. That leads to forming positive connections that focus on deep learning by all, to the ultimate benefit of students.

Advanced teachers advocate and practice sustainable leadership by:

1. Making learning paramount in all leadership activity.

2. Making learning transparent among all educators in the school.

3. Demonstrating evidence-informed leadership through active inquiry into learning.

4. Modeling deep and broad adult learning in their own leadership development and in the kinds of staff development offered to others (Hargreaves & Fink, 2006).

In this way, leadership becomes a distributed or shared process that emphasizes the importance of the interactions that one develops with others and champions roles such as coaching and mentoring (Easton, 2008; Mihans, 2008). Advanced teachers who demonstrate professional leadership are essential to perpetuating and advancing physical education and professional learning in the schools.

Standard 3: Professional Leadership
Advanced physical education teacher candidates (AC) are continuous, collaborative learners who further their own professional development and use their abilities to contribute to the profession.

Element	Unacceptable	Acceptable	Target
3a. Conducts inquiry into professional knowledge and practice and communicates results of inquiry to the profession and community.	AC assesses teaching by thoughtfully considering own practice in relationship to successful practitioners. Results from reflection might be used to improve instruction but are not disseminated to or shared with others.	AC conducts inquiry into professional knowledge and practice. AC shares professional knowledge with colleagues and/or community.	AC questions professional knowledge and practice by conducting formal inquiry into teaching and learning. AC seeks formal means of sharing findings with the profession as a whole and/or advocating for instructional and school improvement.
Element	**Unacceptable**	**Acceptable**	**Target**
3b. Continues personal development through contributions to the growth and professional learning of others.	AC participates in professional learning opportunities for personal benefit.	AC contributes to the improvement of peers', colleagues' or others' practice that leads to the professional learning of all involved.	AC contributes to the development of all involved through sustained formal curricular and/or instructional support to fellow professionals by serving as a mentor or instructional coach, or in other leadership roles.

ASSESSMENTS FOR USE
WITH NASPE'S 2008 STANDARDS FOR ADVANCED PETE

Note: These suggestions for potential sources of evidence are meant for use only as examples. They are neither prescribed nor required assessments, nor do they represent a comprehensive list of the types of evidence that might be used for standards-based assessment.

Standard 1: Professional Knowledge
Advanced physical education teacher candidates (AC) come to understand disciplinary content knowledge, the application of content knowledge to teaching physical education, and modes of inquiry that form the bases for physical education programs and instruction.

Examples of assessments include, but are not limited to, the following:

1. Course grades in disciplinary content, modes and tools of inquiry and pedagogical knowledge.

2. Written or oral comprehensive exams, oral defense.

3. Thesis/thesis proposal, creative component, action research project, literature review.

4. Presentations at professional meetings/conferences.

5. Professional portfolio. Course projects, papers, assignments.

6. Publications.

Standard 2: Professional Practice
Advanced physical education teacher candidates use content knowledge and pedagogical content knowledge to design and conduct appropriate learning experiences that facilitate and enhance the growth of learners.

Examples of assessments include, but are not limited to, the following:

1. Records of live observation and/or captured audio/video performance with analysis and feedback.

2. Lessons and units taught in field settings with results of student assessment, analytical teacher reflection and/or videotape analysis.

3. Thesis, creative component or action research project grounded in questions relevant to teaching practice.

4. Instruments used to solicit preferences, goals, opinions, etc. of candidates' students.

Standard 3: Professional Leadership
Advanced physical education teacher candidates are continuous, collaborative learners who further their own professional development and use their abilities to contribute to the profession.

Examples of assessments include, but are not limited to, the following:

1. Thesis, creative component, action research project.

2. Presentations at professional meetings/conferences.

3. Supervision and/or mentoring of initial candidates, student teachers or new faculty members.

4. Service learning projects within schools or communities at large.

CHARACTERISTICS OF APPROPRIATE ASSESSMENTS OF ADVANCED TEACHER CANDIDATE PERFORMANCE

1. Assessments should contain elements that are also evident in the standard. Concepts in the standards should be apparent in the assessments to the same depth and breadth.

2. At least one focused assessment or a component of an assessment should address each standard. Focused assessments for a few standards are preferred to general assessments that address many standards superficially.

3. Minimal proficiency identified in an assessment's scoring guide should be equal to the expectation established by the standard.

4. All rubrics should provide clear statements to guide judgment when determining the value, worth, or quality of the work presented for evaluation. General scoring guides provide very little direction to evaluators who strive to apply appropriate ratings in a consistent manner across all candidates' work and show high agreement with other evaluators.

5. Scoring rubrics should accompany assessments requiring judgment about the quality of performance/work. Specifically, rubrics should:

    a. Identify important characteristics and make observable distinctions among multiple performance levels.

    b. Provide substantive descriptors that reflect assessments' criteria.

    c. Provide meaningful descriptors reflecting core concepts inherent in the standards.

6. One or more of the assessments collectively should include all key concepts inherent in a standard. Elements identified within each standard provide additional information to help define the scope and depth of appropriate skills, knowledge, and dispositions. Each element within each standard must be assessed.

7. Assessments may be course-based assignments but in all cases they should be drawn from course work required of advanced physical education teacher education candidates. If assessments reside in elective courses, all candidates may not choose those courses.

8. Assessments should reflect performance appropriate to the standards. Key portions of an assessment should be congruent with the intended outcome of an element whether it is knowledge based, practiced in professional settings, or both. If the intended outcome is knowledge and understanding, the assessment or portions of it should focus on the explicit evaluation of knowledge and understanding. If the outcome is application of knowledge and understanding in practice, the assessment's design should allow evaluation of observable behaviors or characteristics demonstrated in authentic settings.

REFERENCES, INITIAL STANDARDS

Standard 1. Scientific and Theoretical Knowledge

Borko, H., Liston, D., & Whitcomb, J. (2006). A conversation of many voices: Critiques and visions of teacher education. *Journal of Teacher Education, 57(3)*, 199-204.

Clark, C. M., & Peterson, P. L. (1986). Teachers' thought processes. In M. C. Wittrock (Ed.), *Handbook of research on teaching*. New York: Macmillan.

Cochran-Smith, M., & Zeichner, K. M. (Eds.). (2005). *Studying teacher education: The report of the AERA panel on research and teacher education*. Mahwah, NJ: LEA Publications.

Darling-Hammond, L. (2006). Constructing 21st-century teacher education. *Journal of Teacher Education, 57(3)*, 300-314.

Darling-Hammond, L., & Bransford, J. (2005). *Preparing teachers for a changing world: What teachers should learn and be able to do*. San Francisco: Jossey-Bass.

Kelly, P., Hickey, C., & Tinning, R. (2000). Producing knowledge about physical education pedagogy: Problemizing the activities of expertise. *Quest, 52(3)*, 284-296.

Kennedy, M. M. (2006). Knowledge and vision in teaching. *Journal of Teacher Education, 57(3)*, 205-211.

Liston, D., Whitcomb, J., & Borko, H. (2006). Too little or too much: Teacher preparation and the first years of teaching. *Journal of Teacher Education, 57(4)*, 351-358.

Rink, J., French, K., Lee, A., Solmon, M., & Lynn, S. (1994). A comparison of pedagogical knowledge structures of preservice students and teacher educators in two institutions. *Journal of Teaching in Physical Education, 13*, 140-162.

Standard 2. Skill-Based and Fitness-Based Competence

Barfield, J.P., Bennett, J., Folio, M. R., & Killman, C. (2007). Disability rights in higher education: Ensuring kinesiology program and accreditation standards do not discriminate. *Quest, 59(4)*, 384-397.

Castelli, D. & Williams, L. (2007). Health-related fitness and physical education teachers content knowledge. *Journal of Teaching in Physical Education, 26(1)*, 3-19.

Chepko, S. F., & Arnold, R. (2000). *Guidelines for physical education programs: Grades K-12 standards, objectives, and assessments*. Boston: Allyn and Bacon.

National Association for Sport and Physical Education. (2004). *Moving Into the future: National standards for physical education* (2nd ed.). Reston, VA: Author.

Peterson, S., Byrne, H., & Cruz, L. (2003). The reality of fitness for pre-service teachers: What physical education majors "know and can do." *The Physical Educator, 60(1)*, 5-18.

Rovegno, I. (1993). Content-knowledge acquisition during undergraduate teacher education: Overcoming cultural templates and learning through practice. *American Educational Research Journal, 30*, 611-642.

Shulman, L. (1986). Paradigms and research agendas in the study of teaching. In M. C. Wittrock (Ed.), *Handbook of research on teaching* (3rd ed., pp. 3-36). New York: Macmillan.

Shulman, L. S. (1987). Knowledge in teaching: Foundations of the new reform. *Harvard Educational Review, 57(1)*, 1-22.

Shulman, L. (2004a). Those who understand: Knowledge growth in teaching. In L. Shulman and S. M. Wilson (Eds.), *The wisdom of practice: Essays on teaching, learning, and learning to teach* (pp. 189-216). San Francisco: Jossey-Bass.

Shulman, L. (2004b). Knowledge and teaching: Foundation of the new reform. In L. Shulman and S. M. Wilson (Eds.), *The wisdom of practice: Essays on teaching, learning, and learning to teach* (pp. 217-248). San Francisco: Jossey-Bass.

Shulman, L. (2004c). Disciplines of inquiry in education. In L. Shulman and S. M. Wilson (Eds.), *The wisdom of practice: Essays on teaching, learning, and learning to teach* (pp. 276-307). San Francisco: Jossey-Bass.

Shulman, L. (2004d). Aristotle had it right. In L. Shulman and S. M. Wilson (Eds.), *The wisdom of practice: Essays on teaching, learning, and learning to teach* (pp. 399-416). San Francisco: Jossey-Bass.

Siedentop, D. (1999). *The context for teacher education: Will PETE be on the inside or outside?* Keynote address presented at the National Association for Sport and Physical Education Physical Education Teacher Education Conference, Bloomingdale, IL.

Siedentop, D. (2002). Content knowledge for physical education. *Journal of Teaching in Physical Education, 21*(4), 368-377.

Tinning, R. (2002). Engaging Siedentopian perspectives on content knowledge for physical education. *Journal of Teaching in Physical Education, 21*(4), 378-391.

Zeigler, E. F. (2003). Guiding professional students to literacy in physical activity education. *Quest, 55*(4), 285-305.

Standard 3. **Planning and Implementation**

Griffey, D. C., & Housner, L. D. (1991). Differences between experienced and inexperienced teachers' planning decisions, interactions, student engagement, and instructional climate. *Research Quarterly for Exercise and Sport, 62*, 196-204.

Griffin, L., Dodds, P., & Rovegno, I. (1996). Pedagogical content knowledge for teachers: Integrate everything you know to help students learn. *Journal of Physical Education, Recreation, and Dance, 67*(9), 58-61.

Housner, L. D. & Griffey, D. C. (1985). Teacher cognition: Differences in planning and interactive decision making between experienced and inexperienced teachers. *Research Quarterly for Exercise and Sport, 56*(1), 45-53.

McCullick, B., Schempp, P., Hsu, S. H., Jung, J. H., Vickers, B., & Schuknecht, G. (2006). An analysis of the working memories of expert sport instructors. *Journal of Teaching in Physical Education, 25*(2), 149-165.

Palmer, S. E., & Hildebrand, K. (2005). Designing appropriate learning tasks: The environmental management model. *Journal of Physical Education, Recreation & Dance, 76*(2), 48-56.

Rink, J. (2004). It's okay to be a beginner. *Journal of Physical Education, Recreation & Dance, 75*(6), 31-34.

Rovegno, I. (1995). Theoretical perspective on knowledge and learning and a student teacher's pedagogical content knowledge of dividing and sequencing subject matter. *Journal of Teaching in Physical Education, 14*, 284-304.

Standard 4. **Instructional Delivery and Management**

Andrew, M. D., Cobb, C. D., & Giampietro, P. J. (2005). Verbal ability and teacher effectiveness. *Journal of Teacher Education, 56*(4), 343-354.

Berliner, D. C. (1986). In pursuit of the expert pedagogue. *Education Researcher, 15*, 5-13.

Berliner, D. C. (1994). Expertise: The wonder of exemplary performances. In J. Mangieri & C. Block (Eds.), *Creating powerful thinking in teachers and students: Diverse perspectives* (pp. 161-186). Fort Worth, TX: Harcourt Brace.

Carter, K., Cushing, K., Sabers, D., Pinnegar, S., & Berliner, D. C. (1987). Processing and using information about students: A study of expert, novice, and postulant teachers. *Teaching and Teacher Education, 3*(2), 147-157.

Carter, K., Cushing, K., Sabers, D., Stein, P., & Berliner, D. C. (1988). Expert-novice differences in perceiving and processing visual classroom information. *Journal of Teacher Education, 39*(3), 25-31.

Dodds, P. (1994). Cognitive and behavioral components of expertise in teaching physical education. *Quest, 46*, 153-163.

Ericsson, K. A. (2003). Development of elite performance and deliberate practice: An update from the perspective of the expert performance approach. In J. L. Starkes & K. A. Ericsson (Eds.), *Expert performance in sports: Advances in research in sport expertise* (pp. 49-83). Champaign, IL: Human Kinetics.

Ericsson, K. A., & Smith, J. (1991). *Toward a general theory of expertise.* Cambridge: Cambridge University Press.

Garrahy, D., Coleman, M., & Jones, D. L. (2005, April). Preservice teacher gender beliefs and practices during an elementary physical education practicum. In R. Gabbei (Chair), *Studying the impact of gender in physical education.* Symposium conducted at the American Alliance for Health, Physical Education, Recreation, and Dance Conference, Chicago, IL.

Garrahy, D. A., Cothran, D. J., & Kulinna, P. H. (2005). Voices from the trenches: An exploration of teachers' management knowledge. *The Journal of Educational Research, 99*(1), 56-58.

Graham, K. C., French, K. E., & Wood, A. M. (1993). Observing and interpreting teaching-learning processes: Novice PETE students, experienced PETE students, and expert teacher educators. *Journal of Teaching in Physical Education, 13*(1), 46-61.

Grenier, M. (2007). Inclusion in physical education: From a medical model to social constructivism. *Quest, 59*(3).

Hyland, N. E. (2005). Understanding diversity through social and community inquiry: An action-research study. *Journal of Teacher Education, 56*(4), 367-381.

Manross, D., & Templeton, C. (1997). Expertise in teaching physical education. *Journal of Physical Education, Recreation, and Dance, 68*(3), 37-41.

McCaughtry, N., & Rovegno, I. (2003). Development of pedagogical content knowledge: Moving from blaming students to predicting skillfulness, recognizing motor development, and understanding emotion. *Journal of Teaching in Physical Education, 22*(4), 355-368.

Owens, L. (2006). Teacher radar: The view from the front of the class. *Journal of Physical Education, Recreation, & Dance, 77*(4), 29-33.

Rovegno, I., Chen, W., & Todorovich, J. (2003). Accomplished teachers' pedagogical content knowledge of teaching dribbling to third grade children. *Journal of Teaching in Physical Education, 22*(4), 246-449.

Schempp, P. G., & Johnson, S. W. (2006). Learning to see: Developing the perception of an expert teacher. *Journal of Physical Education, Recreation & Dance, 77*(6), 29-34.

Schempp, P. G., Manross, D., Tan, S. K. S., & Fincher, M. D. (1998). Subject expertise and teachers' knowledge. *Journal of Teaching in Physical Education, 17*, 342-356.

Schempp, P. G., Tan, S., & McCullick, B. (2002). The practices of expert teachers. *Teaching and Learning, 23,* 99-106.

Smith, T. W., & Strahan, D. (2004). Toward a prototype of expertise in teaching: A descriptive study. *Journal of Teacher Education, 55*(4), 357-371.

Starkes, J. L., Helson, W., & Jack, R. (2001). Expert performance in sport and dance. In R. Singer, C. Janelle, & H. Hausenblas (Eds.), *Handbook of sport psychology* (2nd ed., pp. 174-204). New York: Macmillan.

Standard 5. Impact on Student Learning

Barrett, K. R., & Collie, S. (1996). Children learning lacrosse from teachers learning to teach it: The discovery of pedagogical content knowledge by observing children's movement. *Research Quarterly for Exercise and Sport, 67*(3), 297-309.

Burden, J. W., Jr., Hodge, S. R., O'Bryant, C. P., & Harrison, L., Jr. (2004). From colorblindness to intercultural sensitivity: Infusing diversity training in PETE programs. *Quest, 56*(2), 173-189.

Chen, W., Rovegno, I., Todorovich, J., & Babiarz, M. (2003). Third grade children's movement responses to dribbling tasks presented by accomplished teachers. *Journal of Teaching in Physical Education, 22*(4), 450-466.

Gay, G. (2002). Preparing for culturally responsive teaching. *Journal of Teacher Education, 53*(2), 106-116.

Goodway, J. D. (2002, April). Assessment of preservice teachers using teacher work sample. In S. Stroot (Chair), *Work sample methodology: Assessing the preservice teacher's effectiveness.* Symposium conducted at the meeting of the American Alliance for Health, Physical Education, Recreation, and Dance, San Diego, CA.

Loughran, J. J. (2002). Effective reflective practice: In search of meaning in learning about teaching. *Journal of Teacher Education, 53*(1), 33-43.

Rovegno, I. (1992). Learning to teach in a field-based methods course: The development of pedagogical content knowledge. *Teaching and Teacher Education, 8*(1), 69-82.

Sleeter, C. E. (2001). Preparing teachers for culturally diverse schools: Research and the overwhelming presence of whiteness. *Journal of Teacher Education, 52*(2), 94-106.

Stroot, S. (2002, April). Teacher work sample methodology: A new strategy for physical education teacher education. In S. Stroot, (Chair), *Work sample methodology: Assessing the preservice teacher's effectiveness.* Symposium conducted at the meeting of the American Alliance for Health, Physical Education, Recreation, and Dance, San Diego, CA.

Standard 6. Professionalism

Ferro, J. M. (2000). Reflective practice and professional development. *ERIC Digest.* Retrieved July 11, 2007, from http://www.ericdigests.org/2001-3/reflective.htm.

Hargreaves, A., & Fink, D. (2006). *Sustainable leadership.* San Francisco: Jossey-Bass.

Hutzler, Y. (2003). Attitudes toward the participation of individuals with disabilities in physical activity: A review. *Quest 55*(4), 347-373.

McFalls, E. L., & Cobb-Roberts, D. (2001). Reducing resistance to diversity through cognitive dissonance instruction: Implications for teacher education. *Journal of Teacher Education, 52*(2), 164-172.

O'Sullivan, M., & Deglau, D. (2006). Principles of professional development. *Journal of Teaching in Physical Education, 25,* 441-449.

Rovegno, I. (1994). Teaching within a curricular zone of safety: School culture and the situated nature of student teachers' pedagogical content knowledge. *Research Quarterly in Exercise and Sport, 65(3),* 269-279.

Rovegno, I. & Brandhauer, D. (1997). Psychological dispositions that facilitated and sustained the development of knowledge of a constructivist approach to physical education. *Journal of Teaching in Physical Education, 16(2),* 136-141.

GENERAL REFERENCES

Ayers, S. F., & Griffey, L. D. (2008). A descriptive analysis of undergraduate PETE programs. *Journal of Teaching in Physical Education, 27(1),* 51-67.

Berliner, D.C. (1994). Expertise: The wonder of exemplary performances. In J. Mangieri & C. Block (Eds.), *Creating powerful thinking in teachers and students: Diverse perspectives* (pp. 161-186). Fort Worth, TX: Harcourt Brace College.

Brandon, L.J. & Evans, R.I. (1988). Are physical educators physically fit?: Perceived and measured physical fitness of physical educators. *Journal of Physical Education, Recreation and Dance, 59(7),* 73-75.

Cochran-Smith, M. (2005). Studying teacher education: What we know and need to know. *Journal of Teacher Education, 56(4)* 301-306.

Dotson, C. (1988). Health fitness standards: Aerobic endurance. *Journal of Physical Education, Recreation and Dance, 59(7),* 26-31.

Dyson, B., Griffin, L. L., & Hastie, P. (2004). Sport education, tactical games, and cooperative learning: Theoretical and pedagogical considerations. *Quest, 56(2),* 226-240.

Gore, J. M. (2001). Beyond our differences: A reassembling of what matters in teacher education. *Journal of Teacher Education, 52(2),* 124-135.

Hall, T. J., & Smith, M. A. (2006). Teacher planning, instruction, and reflection: What we know about teacher cognitive processes. *Quest, 58(4).*

Interstate New Teacher Assessment and Support Consortium (1992). *Model standards for beginning teacher licensing, assessment, and development: A resource for state dialogue.* Retrieved September 1, 2006, from http://www.ccsso.org/content/pdfs/corestrd.pdf.

Kirk, D., & Macdonald, D. (2001). The social construction of PETE in higher education: Toward a research agenda. *Quest, 53(4),* 440-456.

Krause, J.V., & Melville, D.S. (1993). Fit for hire-A model for promoting the health and fitness of physical education students. *Journal of Physical Education, Recreation and Dance, 64(4),* 61-65.

Lambert, L. T. (1999). *Standards-based assessment of student learning: A comprehensive approach.* Reston, VA: National Association for Sport and Physical Education.

Lawson, H. A. (1993). Dominant discourses, problem setting, and teacher education pedagogies: A Critique. *Journal of Teaching in Physical Education, 12(2),* 149-160.

Melville, D.S., & Jones, D.M. (1990). Should physical education majors have their fitness levels assessed? *Journal of Physical Education, Recreation and Dance, 61(1),* 30-32.

Mohnsen, B. (2003). *Concepts and principles of physical education: What every student needs to know* (2nd ed.). Reston, VA: National Association for Sport and Physical Education.

Murray, F. B. (2001). The overreliance of accreditors on consensus standards. *Journal of Teacher Education, 52*(3), 211-222.

Murray, F. B. (2005). On building a unified system of accreditation in teacher education. *Journal of Teacher Education, 56*(4), 307-317.

National Association for Sport and Physical Education (1995). *Looking at physical education from a developmental perspective: A guide to teaching.* Reston, VA: Author.

National Association for Sport and Physical Education (2004). *Moving Into the future: National standards for physical education,* 2nd Ed. Reston, VA: Author.

National Association for Sport and Physical Education. (2001). *Standards for advanced programs in physical education teacher education.* Reston, VA: Author.

National Association for Sport and Physical Education. (2007). *What constitutes a highly qualified physical education teacher?* Reston, VA: Author.

National Board for Professional Teaching Standards (2002). *What teachers should know and be able to do.* Retrieved September 1, 2006, from http://www.nbpts.org/resources/publications.

National Council for the Accreditation of Teacher Education (2008). Unit standards. *Professional standards for the accreditation of schools, colleges and departments of education.* Retrieved December 2007 from http://www.ncate.org/public/revisedStds07.asp?ch=4.

Pullin, D. (2004). Accountability, autonomy, and academic freedom in educator preparation programs. *Journal of Teacher Education, 55*(4), 300-312.

Rink, J. (2007). What knowledge is of most worth? Perspectives on kinesiology from pedagogy. *Quest, 59,* 100-110.

Shulman, L. (2004a). Those who understand: Knowledge growth in teaching. In L. Shulman and S. M. Wilson (Eds.), *The wisdom of practice: Essays on teaching, learning, and learning to teach* (pp. 189-216). San Francisco: Jossey-Bass.

Shulman, L. (2004b). Knowledge and teaching: Foundation of the new reform. In L. Shulman and S. M. Wilson (Eds.), *The wisdom of practice: Essays on teaching, learning, and learning to teach* (pp. 217-248). San Francisco: Jossey-Bass.

Shulman, L. (2004c). Disciplines of inquiry in education. In L. Shulman and S. M. Wilson (Eds.), *The wisdom of practice: Essays on teaching, learning, and learning to teach* (pp. 276-307). San Francisco: Jossey-Bass.

Shulman, L. (2004d). Aristotle had it right. In L. Shulman and S. M. Wilson (Eds.), *The wisdom of practice: Essays on teaching, learning, and learning to teach* (pp. 399-416). San Francisco: Jossey-Bass.

Staffo. D. F., & Stier, W. F., Jr. (2000). The use of fitness test in PETE programs. *Journal of Physical Education, Recreation and Dance, 71*(5), 48-52.

Strotsky, S. (2006). Who should be accountable for what beginning teachers need to know? *Journal of Teacher Education, 57*(3), 256-268.

Tamir, E., & Wilson, S. M. (2005). Who should guard the gates? Evidentiary and professional warrants for claiming jurisdiction. *Journal of Teacher Education, 56*(4), 332-342.

Tinning, R. (1991). Teacher education pedagogy: Dominant discourses and the process of problem-setting. *Journal of Teaching Physical Education, 11*(1), 1-20.

Wise, A. E. (2005). Establishing teaching as a profession: The essential role of professional accreditation. *Journal of Teacher Education, 56*(4), 318-331.

REFERENCES, ADVANCED STANDARDS

Berliner, D. C. (1994). Expertise: The wonder of exemplary performances. In J. Mangieri & C. Block (Eds.), *Creating powerful thinking in teachers and students: Diverse perspectives*. Fort Worth, TX: Harcourt Brace.

Clark, C. M., & Peterson, P. L. (1986). Teachers' thought processes. In M. C. Wittrock (Ed.), *Handbook of research on teaching*. New York: Macmillan.

Dodds, P. (1994). Cognitive and behavioral components of expertise in teaching physical education. *Quest, 46*, 153-163.

Easton, L. (2008). From professional development to professional learning. *Phi Delta Kappan, 89* (10), 755-759, 761.

Ferraro, J. M. (2000). Reflective practice and professional development. *ERIC Digest*. Retrieved July 11, 2007, from http://www.ericdigests.org/2001-3/reflective.htm.

Griffin, L., Dodds, P., & Rovegno, I. (1996). Pedagogical content knowledge for teachers: Integrate everything you know to help students learn. *Journal of Physical Education, Recreation, and Dance, 67*(9), 58-61.

Hargreaves, A., & Fink, D. (2006). *Sustainable leadership*. San Francisco: Jossey-Bass.

Hord, S. M. (1997). *Professional learning communities: Communities of continuous inquiry and improvement*. Austin, TX: Southwest Educational Development Laboratory.

Huba, M., & Freed, J. (2000). *Learner-Centered Assessment on College Campuses: Shifting the Focus from Teaching to Learning*. Boston: Allyn & Bacon.

Manross, D., & Templeton, C. (1997). Expertise in teaching physical education. *Journal of Physical Education, Recreation, and Dance, 68*(3), 37-41.

Mihans, R. (2008). Can teachers lead teachers? *Phi Delta Kappan, 89* (10), 762-765.

Mosston, M., & Ashworth, S. (2002). *Teaching Physical Education* (5th ed.). San Francisco: Benjamin Cummings.

National Association for Sport and Physical Education. (2001). *Standards for advanced programs in physical education teacher education*. Retrieved August 15, 2008, from http://www.aahperd.org/naspe/pdf_files/standards_advanced.pdf.

National Association for Sport and Physical Education. (2007). *What constitutes a highly qualified physical education teacher?* Retrieved August 15, 2008, from http://www.aahperd.org/naspe/pdf_files/HiQualified.pdf.

National Council for the Accreditation of Teacher Education. (2008). *Professional standards for the accreditation of teacher preparation institutions*. Retrieved on August 15, 2008, from http://www.ncate.org/public/standards.asp?ch=4.

O'Sullivan, M., & Deglau, D. (2006). Principles of professional development. *Journal of Teaching in Physical Education, 25*, 441-449.

Rink, J., French, K., Lee, A., Solmon, M. & Lynn, S. (1994). A comparison of pedagogical knowledge structures of preservice students and teacher educators in two institutions. *Journal of Teaching in Physical Education, 13*, 140-162.

Rink, J. (2007). What knowledge is of most worth? Perspectives on kinesiology from pedagogy. *Quest, 59*, 100-110.

Rovegno, I. (1995). Theoretical perspectives on knowledge and learning and a student teacher's pedagogical content knowledge of dividing and sequencing subject matter. *Journal of Teaching in Physical Education, 14*, 284-304.

Schempp, P., Manross, D., Tan, S., & Fincher, M. (1998). Subject expertise and teachers' knowledge. *Journal of Teaching in Physical Education, 17*, 342-356.

Shulman, L. (2004a). Those who understand: Knowledge growth in teaching. In L. Shulman and S. M. Wilson (Eds.), *The wisdom of practice: Essays on teaching, learning, and learning to teach* (pp. 189-216). San Francisco: Jossey-Bass.

Shulman, L. (2004b). Knowledge and teaching: Foundation of the new reform. In L. Shulman and S. M. Wilson (Eds.), *The wisdom of practice: Essays on teaching, learning and learning to teach* (pp. 217-248). San Francisco: Jossey-Bass.

Shulman, L. (2004c). Disciplines of inquiry in education. In L. Shulman and S. M. Wilson (Eds.), *The wisdom of practice: Essays on teaching, learning and learning to teach* (pp. 276-307). San Francisco: Jossey-Bass.

Shulman, L. (2004d). Aristotle had it right. In L. Shulman and S. M. Wilson (Eds.), *The wisdom of practice: Essays on teaching, learning, and learning to teach* (pp. 399-416). San Francisco: Jossey-Bass.

Sparks, D. (2003, November). Leaders as creators of high-performance cultures. *Results*. Retrieved June 2, 2007, from http://nsdc.org/library/publications/results/res11-03spar.cfm?pritPage=1&.

Spillane, J. P. (2006). *Distributed leadership*. San Francisco: Jossey-Bass.

GLOSSARY OF TERMS

Advanced Programs*: Post-baccalaureate levels for (1) continuing education for teachers who have previously completed preparation or (2) preparation for other school professionals. Advanced programs commonly award graduate credit and include master's, specialist and doctoral degree programs, as well as non-degree licensure programs at the post-baccalaureate level.

Alignment: Congruence of outcomes, courses/ experiences and assessment activities.

Assessments*: Evaluated activities or tasks that programs or units use to determine the extent to which teacher candidates have mastered specific learning proficiencies, outcomes or standards. Assessments usually include an instrument that details the task or activity and a scoring guide used to evaluate the task or activity. Appropriate assessments in physical education are linked to lesson or unit goals and objectives, are conducted within the context of instruction, and match the developmental level of both the student and teacher candidate.

Collaboration: Interaction and communication with other professionals within and outside the physical education discipline. These interactions ultimately increase opportunities for students and/or reduce barriers related to a physically active lifestyle.

Content Knowledge: In physical education teacher education, content derives from knowledge of movement and knowledge of pedagogy. Knowledge of movement includes mastery of movement forms (e.g., games, sports, dance, aquatics, leisure activities) and information from kinesiology-related areas (e.g., exercise physiology, biomechanics, sport psychology/sociology, motor learning). Knowledge of pedagogy derives from education (e.g., education foundations, instructional technology, general methods) and psychology (e.g., child development, cognitive psychology).

Critical Elements: Essential components of skillful movements. Example: For throwing, the critical elements include arm, body and leg actions.

Developmentally Appropriate: Instruction or activity that is suitable to the learner's level of physical, social, emotional and intellectual development.

Developmentally appropriate instruction accounts for the fact that "developmental change is qualitative, sequential, directional, cumulative, multifactorial and individual" (NASPE, 1995, p. 17).

Disciplinary Knowledge: Foundational information from the knowledge areas of movement and pedagogy that support the field of physical education.

Dispositions*: The attitudes, values and beliefs that educators demonstrate through both verbal and non-verbal behaviors as they interact with students, families, colleagues and communities. These professional dispositions support student learning and development (NCATE, 2008).

Diversity*: Differences among groups of people and individuals based on ethnicity, race, socioeconomic status, gender, exceptionalities, language, religion, sexual orientation, geographical area and/or development.

Exceptionalities*: Physical, mental or emotional conditions — including gifted/talented abilities — that require individualized instruction and/or other education-related support or services.

Health-Enhancing Fitness: Intentional and systematic physical activity that positively enhances the components of personal physical fitness (i.e., cardiovascular and muscular). Improving these components reduces the risk of disease and illness, and enhances overall health and well-being.

Inquiry: Conscious effort to seek answers by posing questions, gathering and analyzing data, drawing conclusions, making inferences or generating hypotheses.

Instructional Cues & Prompts: Verbal cues that direct or focus students' attention to the key elements of a skill or that prompt students to perform key movement components of skills (e.g., "platform with arms" for a volleyball forearm pass.

Instructional Feedback: Specific, intentional, well-timed augmented information that the teacher provides the student that serves the primary purpose of increasing student motor skill learning and performance. Some intentional feedback (used sparingly) also can increase motivation and/or reinforce appropriate behaviors during practice or performance.

Instructional Formats: Teaching approaches ranging from direct to indirect.

Learners: See NCATE definition for *students*.

Learning Experiences: Planned instructional activities designed to help meet learning goals and objectives.

Motor Competency: Competency implies that the teacher demonstrates the activity's fundamental skills and applies those skills effectively in a game situation or performance. Demonstrating competency includes using fundamental game strategies or applying skills to solve advanced movement problems (Chepko & Arnold, 2000, p. 245).

Motor Proficiency: Implies that the learner has mastered advanced skills in game situations or performance. Demonstrating proficiency includes using advanced game strategies, creating movement patterns or creating unique combinations of movements (Chepko & Arnold, 2000, p. 245).

Movement Patterns: Fundamental movements as the essential building blocks to skillful movement. These include locomotor (i.e., jumping and running), non-locomotor (i.e., bending and stretching) and manipulative (i.e., striking and throwing) movement patterns.

Non-Verbal Communication: Techniques of communicating that use expressions, gestures, body posture and/or signals rather than words. Also can include materials, technology and alternative resources such as task cards or poster boards.

Pedagogical Content Knowledge (PCK)*: Interaction of the subject matter and effective teaching strategies to help students learn the subject matter. Requires a thorough understanding of the content to teach it in multiple ways, drawing on students' cultural backgrounds and prior knowledge and experiences.

Pedagogical Knowledge*: The general concepts, theories and research about effective teaching, regardless of content areas.

Performance Assessment*: A comprehensive assessment through which candidates demonstrate their proficiencies in subject, professional and pedagogical knowledge, skills and dispositions, including their abilities to exert positive effects on student learning.

Performance Concepts: Knowledge and action concepts related to skillful performance of movement and fitness activities. Includes the aspects of (1) correct *selection* or "what" to do when performing a skill (i.e., when to choose a drop shot or why to choose low repetitions for strength training); and (2) correct *execution* or "how" to do a skill (i.e., executing a wrist flick or the speed of lowering the weight in a repetition) (Rink, 2003).

Personal Competence in Motor Performance: The teacher candidate demonstrates movement skill and movement patterns at a level necessary to perform a variety of physical activities. Teacher candidates are expected to be at least minimally competent in many movement forms and proficient in a few movement forms (NASPE, 2004). Teacher preparation programs can assess teacher candidates' personal competence of in a variety of ways.

Personal Competence in Health-Enhancing Fitness: The teacher candidate demonstrates that he or she is physically fit and participates regularly in physical activity that enhances personal fitness and overall health (NASPE, 2004). Teacher preparation programs can assess teacher candidates' achievement and maintenance of health-enhancing levels of physical fitness in a variety of ways.

Physically Educated Individuals: See Note 3 on p. 58.

Portfolio*: An accumulation of evidence about individual proficiencies, especially in relation to explicit standards and rubrics, used to evaluate competency as a teacher or in another professional school role. Contents might include end-of-course evaluations and tasks used for instructional or clinical experience purposes, such as projects, journals and faculty observations, videos, comments by cooperating teachers or internship supervisors, and samples of student work.

Professional Development*: Opportunities for professional education faculty to develop new knowledge and skills through in-service education, conference attendance, sabbatical leave, summer leave, or inter-instructional visitations, fellowships and work in P-12 schools, etc.

Professional Dispositions*: Professional attitudes, values, and beliefs demonstrated through both verbal and non-verbal behaviors as educators interact with students, families, colleagues, and communities. These positive behaviors support student learning and development.

Professional Learning: Changes in practice resulting from a culture of inquiry and reflection in an ongoing collaborative environment among all involved in the school setting (Easton, 2008).

Reflection: Mental process in which teacher candidates consider relevant instruction and context-related factors (i.e., student diversity, developmental differences, motor skill type), student learning outcome achievement and assessment data to modify instruction and enhance future student learning.

Reflective Cycle: The systematic and comprehensive process of using assessment data to inform the teacher candidate about students' learning outcomes achievement and modifying instruction (based on assessment data) to enhance student learning.

Short- and Long-Term Plans: For Initial Standards, short-term plans refer to daily lesson plans; long-term plans refer to unit plans (weeks or collection of daily lessons). Daily lesson plans comprise unit plans. For Advanced Standards, short-term plans refer to daily and unit lesson plans; long-term plans refer to yearly or curriculum/program plans.

Students*: Children and youths attending P-12 schools, as distinguished from teacher candidates.

Teacher Candidates*: Individuals admitted to, or enrolled in, programs for initial teacher preparation, teachers continuing their professional development or other professional school personnel. Candidates are distinguished from students in P-12 schools.

Technology*: What teacher candidates must know and understand about using information technology to work effectively with students and professional colleagues in (1) delivering, developing, prescribing and assessing instruction; (2) problem-solving; (3) school and classroom administration; (4) education research; (5) electronic information access and exchange; and (6) personal and professional productivity.

Variety of Physical Activities: Specific motor skills and activities that, together, constitute P-12 physical education. Can include but are not limited to: aquatics, dance and rhythm, fitness activities, fundamental motor skills, lifetime leisure activities, outdoor activities and sports (team, individual and dual).

---

* Definitions adapted from and used with permission from the National Council for Accreditation of Teacher Education (NCATE).

Notes:

1. Readers should familiarize themselves thoroughly with the Glossary of NCATE Terms, as found in the NCATE Unit Standards in Professional Standards for the Accreditation of Schools, Colleges, and Departments of Education, found at http://www.ncate.org/public/standards.asp.

2. Throughout the standards and elements, the term teacher candidate refers to pre-service teachers in an initial preparation program. The term advanced candidate refers to candidates in a master's degree or post-initial licensure program. The term student refers to the school-age (K-12) student.

3. Throughout the standards and outcomes, the term physically educated individuals refers to NASPE's (2004) definition of a physically educated person:

   • Has learned skills necessary to perform a variety of physical activities.

   • Knows the implications of and the benefits of involvement in physical activities.

   • Participates regularly in physical activity.

   • Is physically fit.

   • Values physical activity and its contribution to a healthy lifestyle.

2008 Standards & Elements	2001 Standards & Outcomes
Standard 1	
Element 1.1	Similar to 2001 Outcome 1.3
Element 1.2	New with the 2008 Standards
Element 1.3	New with the 2008 Standards
Element 1.4	Similar to 2001 Outcome 1.4
Element 1.5	Similar to 2001 Outcome 1.1
Standard 2	
Element 2.1	Similar to 2001 Outcome 1.2 (FYI: Aligns with NASPE K-12 PE Standard 1)
Element 2.2	New (FYI: Aligns with NASPE K-12 Standard 4)
Element 2.3	New. This is a candidate performance-based expectation somewhat aligned with 2001 Outcome 1.3 (FYI: Somewhat aligns with NASPE K-12 PE Standard 2)
Standard 3	
Element 3.1	Similar to 2001 Outcome 6.2
Element 3.2	Similar to 2001 Outcomes 1.6 and 6.1
Element 3.3	Similar to intent of a variety of 2001 outcomes
Element 3.4	Similar to 2001 Outcomes 3.2, 4.2 and 6.7
Element 3.5	Similar to 2001 Outcomes 2.1, 2.3, 3.1 and 6.3
Element 3.6	Similar to 2001 Outcomes 2.3, 3.1 and 6.3
Element 3.7	Similar to 2001 Standard 9, Technology. Specifically aligns with 2001 Outcomes 9.1 and 9.2
Standard 4	
Element 4.1	Similar to 2001 Standard 5, Communication, specifically Outcomes 5.1 and 5.2.
Element 4.2	Remotely similar to 2001 Outcomes 6.8 and 6.9
Element 4.3	Remotely aligns with the intent of 2001 Outcome 7.2
Element 4.4	New with the 2008 Standards
Element 4.5	Remotely aligns with 2001 Outcome 4.1
Element 4.6	Similar to 2001 Outcome 4.4 (FYI: Aligns with NASPE K-12 PE Standard 5)
Standard 5	
Element 5.1	Similar to 2001 Outcome 7.2
Element 5.2	Similar to 2001 Outcome 7.2
Element 5.3	Similar to 2001 Standard 8, Reflection. Specifically, Outcomes 8.1 and 8.3.
Standard 6	
Element 6.1	New with the 2008 Standards
Element 6.2	Similar to 2001 Outcome 10.2
Element 6.3	New with the 2008 Standards
Element 6.4	Similar to 2001 Outcome 5.3

Appendix A: 2001 & 2008 Initial Standards Alignment Chart

APPENDIX B:
ASSIGNMENT, SCORING GUIDE AND DATA TABLE SAMPLES

Reflection Assessment
Provided by Department of Physical Education, Sport and Human Performance, Winthrop University

Reflection Assignment

Teachers' ability to develop as reflective practitioners is one of the key elements of effective teaching. Ongoing reflection regarding content, instructional practices, assessment data and teaching effectiveness is essential to professional growth. Reflection allows teacher candidates to use the reflective cycle to improve teaching effectiveness. The reflective cycle requires teachers to critically evaluate their teaching effectiveness, reflect on changes to be made for the next lesson to improve effectiveness and implement the changes based on the reflection. The reflective cycle then repeats itself for the next lesson.

Components

After each teaching experience, you will complete a typed reflection on the experience. Each reflection must include the following elements:

1. Describe the class's context or teaching environment. Consider factors such as the number of students in the class, the teaching environment, which can influence instruction decisions, the diversity of abilities among students, the amount of equipment available and any contextual factors that might affect teaching effectiveness.

2. Analyze/justify your teaching performance. Provide an in-depth analysis of your teaching experience, including justifying your instruction decisions (selecting objectives, task sequence, selecting learning experiences, etc.). Address the lesson's developmental appropriateness and the management techniques (routines, procedures and transitions) you use. Be sure to cite specific examples or assessment data to support your observations in the reflection.

3. Critique your performance. Reflect on how effective you were in meeting the objectives for the class and discuss why you did or did not meet your objectives. Support all observations with specific examples. Describe assessments you used to determine whether you met your objectives. Reflect on the various teaching approaches used during the lesson and how the approaches selected were congruent with the lesson's objectives. Describe how you determined the lesson's impact on student learning.

4. Describe in the final section how you will use what you have learned from this lesson in planning and implementing the next lesson. Include a detailed application of lessons learned, and support proposed changes with assessment data (informal or formal). Changes could include using a different teaching approach, adjusting unit goals, changing management routines or adjusting instruction delivery.

Reflection Scoring Guide

Provided by Department of Physical Education, Sport and Human Performance, Winthrop University

Traits (Weight)	Completeness of Reflection/Context	Analysis/Justification of Teaching Performance	Critique of Teaching Performance	Application/ Implementation for Change	Written Communication
4 pts. (Target)	Consistently supports observation with specific examples. Thorough and complete description of the context of the observation. Answers the question of who was in the class and identifies key contextual elements.	In-depth analysis of the teaching experience, including a complete justification of planned learning experiences, objectives for the lessons and task sequence. Reflects on the developmental appropriateness of the learning experiences, sequence of the lesson and transitions.	Interpretations of teaching performance are insightful and based on the observation. Reflects on how lesson objectives were met or not met and gives specific examples to support reflection based on assessments used in the lesson. Reflects on teaching approaches used during the lesson and the alignment of teaching approach and objectives for the lesson.	Provides conclusive and detailed applications, with concrete plans for change that include specific teaching goals. Bases applications on authentic assessments used during the teaching episode. Provides a detailed description of how assessments were used to formulate teaching goals.	Written exceptionally well, with no mistakes in grammar or punctuation.
3 pts. (Acceptable)	Usually supports observation with specific examples. Adequate description of the context of the observation. Answers the question of who was in the class and identifies at least two contextual elements.	Appropriate analysis of the teaching experience including justification of the planned learning experiences, objectives for the lessons and the developmental appropriateness of the learning experiences.	Interpretations of teaching performance are accurate and based on the observable behavior. Reflects on how lesson objectives were met or not met, but no specific examples are given to support reflection. Reflects on assessments used in lesson to determine impact on student learning.	Informed and detailed applications are provided with generalized plans for change and at least one specific teaching goal. Applications are based on teacher's perceptions of student achievement and not any assessment. Provides a general description of how assessments were used to formulate teaching goals.	Written well, with fewer than five mistakes in grammar or punctuation that interfere with reading the reflection.

Continued

2 pts. (Unacceptable)	Sometimes supports observation with specific examples. Brief description of the context of the observation. Answers the question of who was in the class and identifies at least one contextual element.	Surface analysis of the teaching experience including a limited justification of the planned learning experiences. Reflection does not include analysis of the developmental appropriateness of the objectives or the learning experiences.	Interpretations of teaching performance include some misconceptions, and reflective statements are not supported by observable behavior. Reflects either on how the objectives were met or not met, but not both. Doesn't include how assessments were used in the lesson to determine impact on student learning.	Provides generalized applications with generalized plans for change and at least one specific goal identified. Applications are not based on any assessment of student achievement.	Written poorly, but with fewer than 10 mistakes in grammar and punctuation that interfere with reading the reflection.
1 pt. (Unacceptable)	Rarely or never supports observation with specific examples. Incomplete description of the context of the observation. Does not answer, who was in the class.	Little or no analysis and/or no justification of the teaching performance.	No interpretations of teaching performance are made. Does not reflect on how objectives were met or not met.	No applications, plans or teaching goals are included. Applications are not based on any assessment of student achievement.	Written poorly, with more than 10 mistakes in grammar and punctuation that interfere with reading the refection.

UNDERGRADUATE					
Course	**Semester**	**N**	**% TCs Unacceptable**	**% TCs Acceptable**	**% TCs Target**
PHED 348 Elem. Methods	Fall 2008	4	0% (0/4)	75% (3/4)	25% (1/4)
PHED 391 Secondary Methods	Spring 2009	12	0% (0/12)	67% (8/12)	33% (4/12)
PHED 350 Adapted PE	Fall 2008	8	0% (0/8)	75% (6/8)	25% (2/8)
PHED 394 Fieldwork	Fall 2008	4	0% (0/4)	25% (1/4)	75% (3/4)
*EDUC 475 Internship	Fall 2008 Spring 2009	6	0% (0/6)	33% (2/6)	67% (4/6)
	Totals	34	0% (0/34)	59% (20/34)	41% (14/34)

*All candidates must score at the Acceptable level or above in EDUC 475 to meet the standard. Scores are kept in other courses to measure candidate progress.

- **Target** level = between **17 and 20 points** on the rubric.

- **Acceptable** level = between **14 and 16 points** on the rubric.

- **Unacceptable** level = **13 points** or fewer.

Teacher candidates begin reflecting after each teaching episode, using the reflection rubric in their first year in the program. By the time candidates are formally accepted into teacher education program (junior year) and enroll in courses at 300 level and above, they have mastered reflection. This accounts for all candidates' scoring at the Acceptable level and above on reflection. Candidates' individual scores on reflection are calculated by adding all reflection scores for the semester and determining the average score per candidate.

Data Chart for Reflection Rubric

Provided by Department of Physical Education, Sport and Human Performance, Winthrop University

GRADUATE MAT PROGRAM					
Course	Semester	N	% TCs Unacceptable	% TCs Acceptable	% TCs Target
PHED 670 Elem. Methods	Fall 2008	0	0%	0%	0%
PHED 671 Secondary Methods	Spring 2009	11	0% (0/11)	64% (7/11)	36% (4/11)
PHED 662 Adapted PE	Fall 2008	10	20% (2/10)	80% (8/10)	0% (0/10)
PHED 692 Fieldwork	Fall 2008	3	0% (0/3)	33% (1/3)	67% (2/3)
*EDUC 690 Internship	Fall 2008 Spring 2009	2	0% (0/2)	50% (1/2)	50% (1/2)
	Totals	26	8% (2/26)	65% (17/26)	27% (7/26)

*All candidates must score at the acceptable level or above in EDUC 690 to meet the standard. Scores are kept in other courses to measure candidate progress.

- **Target** level = between **17 and 20 points** on the rubric.

- **Acceptable** level = between **14 and 16 points** on the rubric.

- **Unacceptable** level = **13 points** and fewer.

MAT candidates initially use the reflection rubric in PHED 662 – Adapted Physical Education. Their scores tend to be lower initially than those of undergraduates, because this their first experience reflecting on their teaching. Candidates' individual scores on reflection are calculated by adding all reflection scores for the semester and determining the average score per candidate.

Teacher candidates (TC) will be evaluated on their ability to competently perform basic skills (Element 2.1) and performance concepts (Element 2.3) needed to play invasion sports (soccer and lacrosse). Skillfulness and performance concepts will be evaluated while TCs participate in the authentic environment (modified games with 7 members per team). TCs who cannot participate in the authentic environment with 7 players, at game speed, may participate in a modified game (consists of 3 v. 3 game at reduced speed). The scoring guide used to assess skillfulness and performance concepts is attached.

The minimum level of acceptable performance (Level 3, Acceptable) in each category aligns with the highest level of performance needed to demonstrate skills or performance concepts for teaching soccer and lacrosse in the K-12 physical education environment. TCs must achieve at the acceptable level of performance (Level 3, Acceptable) in all categories to receive a passing score on this assignment. The TC must achieve a passing score on this assignment in order to pass the course.

The assignment will be administered during a scheduled class time near the end of the semester (see "tentative schedule" on syllabus for date). As such, attendance is mandatory for the date of this assignment in order to be eligible to receive a grade for it.

Skills (Aligns with NASPE Element 2.1)

Soccer

The skills to be evaluated during game play include kicking, trapping and dribbling.

Criteria for acceptable kicking: TC executes skill, at game speed, competently in the authentic environment (in a game of at least 7 v. 7 of equal or better teammates and competitors). While traveling, TC kicks a moving ball to a teammate so it arrives within one step in any direction surrounding the teammate or the ball is kicked to the space a teammate is traveling toward and the ball arrives just ahead or just after the teammate.

Criteria for acceptable trapping: TC executes the skill, at game speed, competently in the authentic environment (in a game of at least 7 v. 7 of equal or better teammates and competitors). TC traps a moving ball with the dominant foot efficiently every time.

Criteria for acceptable dribbling: TC executes the skill, at game speed, competently in the authentic environment (in a game of at least 7 v. 7 of equal or better teammates and competitors). TC dribbles past 1 defender with control and ends with an accurate pass to teammate or shot on goal.

Lacrosse

The skills to be evaluated during game play include throwing, catching and cradling.

Criteria for acceptable throwing: TC executes the throw, at game speed, competently in the authentic environment (in a game of at least 7 v. 7 of equal or better teammates and competitors). While traveling, TC throws a ball accurately to a teammate so it arrives within one step in any direction surrounding the teammate or the ball is thrown to the space a teammate is traveling toward and the ball arrives just ahead or just after the teammate.

Criteria for acceptable catching: TC catches the lacrosse ball, at game speed, competently in the authentic environment (in a game of at least 7 v. 7 of equal or better teammates and competitors). TC catches a thrown ball with the dominant hand efficiently every time without dropping it and ready to pass or shoot.

Criteria for acceptable cradling: TC cradles the ball competently in the authentic environment (in a game of at least 7 v. 7 of equal or better teammates and competitors). TC cradles while traveling at game speed past 1 defender with control (control is such that defense cannot gain possession by checking and ball stays in pocket) and ends with a pass to a teammate or shot on goal.

Performance Concepts (Aligns with NASPE Element 2.3)

Soccer and Lacrosse

The performance concepts that will be evaluated during game play are guarding/marking and ability to adjust from offense to defense.

Criteria for acceptable guarding/marking: TC guards/marks an attacking opponent and usually forces the opponent to a sideline, forcing the opponent to complete a pass that does not gain yardage or loses yardage. TC implements the following cues when guarding/marking an opponent (in a game of at least 7 v. 7 of equal or near-equal teammates and competitors):

- Closes the space. TC reduces the space the opponent can use to travel with the ball and gain yardage toward goal.

- Positions to force the ball sideways. TC uses his/her body to deny a forward pass and TC forces opponent with the ball to pass backward and lose yardage or pass sideways to maintain but not gain yardage.

Criteria for acceptable ability to adjust: TC adjusts quickly when team moves from defense to offense. TC implements the following cues when adjusting or transitioning from defense to offense (in a game of at least 7 v. 7 of equal or near-equal teammates and competitors):

- Quick moves. TC changes speed and direction, as needed. (Examples: TC might have been jogging to move with the ball on opposite side of field or marking an opponent and now sprints toward his/her goal; TC may have been traveling side-to-side while marking an opponent and now moves toward his/her goal.)

- Field positioning. TC often cuts wide to give teammate with the ball a passing option. TC attempts to beat a defender using body fake, dodge, speed or combination to remain open for a pass.

- Communication. TC tells teammate with the ball that he/she is open to receive a pass, if needed. TC continues to communicate if a defender positions him/herself between ball and TC.

SCORING GUIDE FOR SKILLS

SPORT: SOCCER

Skill	Level
Kicking (Element 2.1)	**Level 4 (Target)** TC kicks proficiently in the authentic environment (in a game of 7 v. 7 of equal or near-equal teammates and competitors). While traveling at game speed, TC kicks a moving ball accurately to a teammate or to the space the teammate is moving toward to receive the ball. (See glossary for definition of motor proficiency.)
	Level 3 (Acceptable) TC kicks competently in the authentic environment (in a game of at least 7 v. 7 of equal or better teammates and competitors). While traveling at game speed, TC kicks a moving ball to a teammate so it arrives within one step in any direction surrounding a teammate, or kicks the ball to the space a teammate is traveling toward and the ball arrives just ahead or just after the teammate. (See glossary for definition of motor competency.)
	Level 2 (Unacceptable) TC cannot consistently* kick the ball with accuracy, but attempts to do so in the authentic environment (in a game of at least 7 v. 7 of teammates and competitors of equal or better skill and tactical performance). While traveling, TC does not kick a moving ball to a teammate with timing and accuracy so the ball arrives just ahead or just after the teammate and ball is consistently out of reach. (*Defined throughout the rubric as at least 85% of the time.)
	Level 1 (Unacceptable) TC cannot kick the ball, at game speed, in the authentic environment (in a game of at least 3 v. 3 of teammates and competitors of equal or better skill and tactical performance). TC must play in a modified game at a slower speed in order to attempt to perform the skills. Sometimes in the modified game TC can kick and sometimes there are errors.
	Level 0 (Unacceptable) TC cannot or will not kick a moving soccer ball during game play.
Trapping (Element 2.1)	**Level 4 (Target)** TC traps the soccer ball proficiently in the authentic environment (in a game of at least 7 v. 7 of equal or near-equal teammates and competitors). TC traps a moving ball with dominant and non-dominant foot consistently and efficiently and with ball in a ready position for passing.
	Level 3 (Acceptable) TC traps the ball competently in the authentic environment (in a game of at least 7 v. 7 of equal or better teammates and competitors). TC traps a moving ball with the dominant foot consistently and efficiently with ball in a ready position for passing.
	Level 2 (Unacceptable) TC cannot consistently trap the ball, but attempts to do so in the authentic environment (in a game of at least 7 v. 7 of teammates and competitors of equal or better skill and tactical performance). TC inconsistently traps a moving ball with the dominant foot and ball is not in a ready position for passing.
	Level 1 (Unacceptable) TC cannot trap the ball in the authentic environment (in a game of at least 3 v. 3 of teammates and competitors of equal or better skill and tactical performance). TC must play in a modified game at a slower speed in order to attempt to perform the skills. Occasionally, in the modified game, TC can trap the ball.
	Level 0 (Unacceptable) TC cannot or will not trap a moving soccer ball during game play.

Continued

Dribbling (Element 2.1)	**Level 4 (Target)** TC dribbles proficiently in the authentic environment (in a game of at least 7 v. 7 of equal or near-equal teammates and competitors). TC dribbles through at least 3 different defenders with control, at game speed (control is such that defense cannot gain possession), and ends with an accurate pass to a teammate or a shot on goal.
	Level 3 (Acceptable) TC executes the dribble competently in the authentic environment (in a game of at least 7 v. 7 of equal or better teammates and competitors). TC dribbles, at game speed, past 1 defender with control and ends with accurate pass to teammate or shot on goal.
	Level 2 (Unacceptable) TC cannot consistently dribble but attempts to do so in the authentic environment (in a game of at least 7 v. 7 of teammates and competitors of equal or better skill and tactical performance). TC inconsistently dribbles past 1 defender, resulting in an inaccurate or reduced speed pass or shot on goal.
	Level 1 (Unacceptable) TC cannot dribble in the authentic environment (in a game of at least 3 v. 3 of teammates and competitors of equal or better skill and tactical performance). TC plays in a modified game at a slower speed in order to attempt to demonstrate dribbling. Sometimes in the modified game the TC can perform the skills and sometimes there are errors. TC cannot dribble past 1 defender with control or end with an accurate pass to a teammate or shot on goal.
	Level 0 (Unacceptable) TC cannot or will not dribble soccer ball during game play.

SPORT: LACROSSE	
Skill	**Level**
Throwing (Element 2.1)	**Level 4 (Target)** TC proficiently executes the throw at game speed in the authentic environment (in a game of at least 7 v. 7 of equal or near-equal teammates and competitors). While traveling at game speed, TC throws a ball accurately, using dominant and non-dominant hands, to a teammate who is cutting to space to receive the ball.
	Level 3 (Acceptable) TC competently executes the throw at game speed in the authentic environment (in a game of at least 7 v. 7 of equal or near-equal teammates and competitors). While traveling, TC throws a ball accurately with the dominant hand to a teammate so it arrives within one step in any direction surrounding the teammate, or the ball is thrown to the space a teammate is traveling toward and the ball arrives just ahead or just after the teammate.
	Level 2 (Unacceptable) TC cannot consistently perform the throw, at game speed, but attempts to do so in the authentic environment (in a game of at least 7 v. 7 of teammates and competitors of equal or near-equal skill and tactical performance). While traveling, TC throws a ball with minimal accuracy using the dominant hand to a teammate so it arrives within one or two steps in any direction surrounding the teammate.
	Level 1 (Unacceptable) TC cannot throw the ball at game speed in the authentic environment (in a game of at least 3 v. 3 of teammates and competitors of equal or near-equal skill and tactical performance). TC must play in a modified game at a slower speed in order to attempt to throw the ball. Sometimes in the modified game TC can throw and sometimes there are errors. While traveling, TC throws a ball with minimal accuracy to a teammate so it arrives within one or two steps in any direction surrounding the teammate.
	Level 0 (Unacceptable) TC cannot or will not throw a lacrosse ball using the lacrosse stick during game play.

Continued

Catching (Element 2.1)	**Level 4 (Target)** TC consistently and proficiently catches the lacrosse ball at game speed in the authentic environment (in a game of at least 7 v. 7 of equal or near-equal teammates and competitors). While cutting to space at game speed, TC catches a thrown ball with dominant and non-dominant hands, quickly and in a ready position for passing or shooting.
	Level 3 (Acceptable) TC catches the lacrosse ball competently at game speed, in the authentic environment (in a game of at least 7 v. 7 of equal or better teammates and competitors). TC catches a thrown ball with the dominant hand without dropping it and ready to pass or shoot within two steps.
	Level 2 (Unacceptable) TC can't catch the ball consistently when playing at game speed, but attempts to do so in the authentic environment (in a game of at least 7 v. 7 of teammates and competitors of equal or near-equal skill and tactical performance). TC doesn't catch a thrown ball with the dominant hand consistently while moving. TC stops to catch the ball with the dominant hand, and the resulting pass or shot is from a stationary position.
	Level 1 (Unacceptable) TC can't catch the lacrosse ball at game speed in the authentic environment (in a game of at least 3 v. 3 of teammates and competitors of equal or near-equal skill and tactical performance). TC must play in a modified game at a slower speed to attempt to catch the ball. Sometimes, in the modified game, the TC can catch; sometimes, he/she makes errors (e.g., doesn't catch a thrown ball with the dominant hand efficiently every time without dropping it and being ready to pass or shoot).
	Level 0 (Unacceptable) TC cannot or will not attempt to catch a lacrosse ball when in a game.
Cradling (Element 2.1)	**Level 4 (Target)** TC consistently cradles the ball proficiently in the authentic environment (in a game of at least 7 v. 7 of equal or near-equal teammates and competitors). TC cradles while traveling at game speed past at least 3 different defenders with control (control is such that defense cannot gain possession by checking and ball stays in pocket) and ends with accurate pass to a teammate or shot on goal.
	Level 3 (Acceptable) TC consistently cradles the ball competently in the authentic environment (in a game of at least 7 v. 7 of equal or near-equal teammates and competitors). TC cradles while traveling at game speed past 1 defender with control (control is such that defense cannot gain possession by checking and ball stays in pocket) and ends with a pass to a teammate or shot on goal.
	Level 2 (Unacceptable) TC cannot consistently cradle the ball while traveling at game speed, but attempts to do so in the authentic environment (in a game of at least 7 v. 7 of teammates and competitors of equal or near-equal skill and tactical performance). TC is able to cradle, but is not consistent each time of possession. TC does not consistently cradle while traveling past 1 defender.
	Level 1 (Unacceptable) TC cannot cradle in the authentic environment (in a game of at least 3 v. 3 of teammates and competitors of equal or near-equal skill and tactical performance). TC must play in a modified game at a slower speed in order to attempt to cradle the ball. Sometimes in the modified game the TC can perform the skills and sometimes there are errors (does not cradle while traveling past 1 defender).
	Level 0 (Unacceptable) TC cannot or will not attempt to cradle a lacrosse ball when in a game.

SPORTS: SOCCER and LACROSSE

Performance Concept	Level
Guard/Mark (Element 2.3)	**Level 4 (Target)** TC consistently channels attacking opponents to a sideline, forcing the opponent to complete a pass that does not gain yardage or loses yardage. TC implements the following cues when channeling opponents in the authentic environment (in a game of at least 7 v. 7 of equal or near-equal teammates and competitors): • Closes the space. TC reduces the space the opponent can use to travel with the ball and gain yardage toward goal. • Positions oneself to force the ball sideways. TC uses his/her body to deny a forward pass and TC forces opponent with the ball to pass backward and lose yardage or pass sideways to maintain but not gain yardage. • Slide and drop back. TC uses quick feet to move sideways and backward in a defensive position (defensive position = body angled forward at the waist, eyes tracking player and ball, maintaining speed with opponent and communicating with teammates) with opponent as body is positioned to deny forward space at about a 45 degree angle with opponent; TC maintains balance, pace, can change direction as opponent may change direction. **Level 3 (Acceptable)** TC is able to guard or mark an attacking opponent and usually channels the opponent to a sideline, forcing the opponent to complete a pass that does not gain yardage or loses yardage. TC implements the following cues when guarding or marking an opponent (in a game of at least 7 v. 7 of equal or near-equal teammates and competitors): • Closes the space. TC reduces the space the opponent can use to travel with the ball and gain yardage toward goal. • Positions to force the ball sideways. TC uses his/her body to deny a forward pass and TC forces opponent with the ball to pass backward and lose yardage or pass sideways to maintain but not gain yardage. • Slides and drops back. TC uses quick feet to move sideways and backward in a defensive position (body angled forward at the waist, eyes tracking player and ball and communicating with teammates) with opponent, as body is positioned to deny forward space at about a 45-degree angle with opponent. TC maintains balance and pace, can change direction as opponent changes direction. Sometimes, the opponent beats TC, if the opponent is very fast and TC is of average speed. **Level 2 (Unacceptable)** TC can't consistently guard or mark an opponent to channel the opponent to the sideline, which is intended to force the opponent to complete a pass that gains no yardage or loses yardage. TC implements some skills, as described below, when guarding or marking an opponent at game speed but is not consistent each time and often is beat by the opponent or allows the opponent to complete a pass that gains yardage (in a game of at least 7 v. 7 of equal or near-equal teammates and competitors). • Closes the space. TC reduces the space the opponent can use to travel with the ball and gain yardage toward the goal. • Positions to force the ball sideways. TC uses his/her body to deny a forward pass and forces opponent with the ball to pass backward and lose yardage, or pass sideways to maintain yardage but not gain any. • Slides and drops back. TC uses quick feet to move sideways and backward in a defensive position (body angled forward at the waist, eyes tracking opponent and ball, and communicating with teammates), with body positioned at about a 45-degree angle to opponent to deny forward advance. TC maintains balance and pace, and can change direction with opponent. TC is beat sometimes if the opponent is very fast and TC is of average speed.

Continued

Guard/Mark (Element 2.3) (*Cont.*)	**Level 1 (Unacceptable)** TC can't perform the following skills at game speed in the authentic environment (in a game of at least 3 v. 3 of teammates and competitors of equal or near-equal skill and tactical performance). The TC must play in a modified game at a slower speed in order to attempt to perform the skills. Sometimes in the modified game the TC can perform the skills and sometimes there are errors. • Closes the space. TC reduces the space the opponent can use to travel with the ball and gain yardage toward goal. • Positions to force the ball sideways. TC uses his/her body to deny a forward pass and TC forces opponent with the ball to pass backward and lose yardage or pass sideways to maintain but not gain yardage. • Slides and drops back. TC uses quick feet to move sideways and backward in a defensive position (body angled forward at the waist, eyes tracking player and ball and communicating with teammates) with opponent, as body is positioned to deny forward space at about a 45-degree angle with opponent. TC maintains balance and pace, can change direction as opponent may change direction. Sometimes, the opponent beats TC, if the opponent is very fast and TC is of average speed.
	Level 0 (Unacceptable) TC does not attempt to perform the following skills in the authentic environment at game speed or in a modified game at a slower speed (game is of at least 3 v. 3 and competitors are of equal or near-equal skill and tactical performance). • Closes the space. TC reduces the space the opponent can use to travel with the ball and gain yardage toward goal. • Positions to force the ball sideways. TC uses his/her body to deny a forward pass and forces opponent to pass backward and lose yardage or pass sideways to maintain but not gain yardage. • Slides and drops back. TC uses quick feet to move sideways and backward in a defensive position (body angled forward at the waist, eyes tracking player and ball and communicating with teammates) with opponent, as body is positioned to deny forward space at about a 45-degree angle with opponent. TC maintains balance and pace, can change direction as opponent may change direction. Sometimes, the opponent beats TC, if the opponent is very fast and TC is of average speed.
Adjust (Element 2.3)	**Level 4 (Target)** TC consistently transitions from defense to offense when a teammate gains possession. TC is continually aware and therefore adjusts personal positioning on the field whenever there is a change in possession. TC implements the following cues when adjusting from defense to offense in the authentic environment (in a game of at least 7 v. 7 of equal or near-equal teammates and competitors): • Quick moves. TC changes speed and direction quickly, as needed. (Examples: TC might have been jogging to move with the ball on opposite side of field or marking an opponent and now sprints toward his/her goal; TC may have been traveling side-to-side while marking an opponent and now moves toward his/her goal.) • Field positioning. TC often cuts wide to give teammate with the ball a passing option. If a teammate is already in position for a wide pass on TC's strong side, TC may spring forward to receive a deep forward pass or stay behind ball for a back pass, if needed. TC attempts to beat a defender using body fake, dodge, speed or combination to remain open for a pass. • Communication. TC tells teammate with the ball that he/she is open to receive a pass, if needed. TC continues to communicate if a defender positions him/herself between ball and TC.

Continued

Adjust (Element 2.3) (*Cont.*)	**Level 3 (Acceptable)** TC is able to adjust quickly when team moves from defense to offense. TC implements the following cues when adjusting or transitioning from defense to offense (in a game of at least 7 v. 7 of equal or near-equal teammates and competitors): • Quick moves. TC changes speed and direction, as needed. (Examples: TC might have been jogging to move with the ball on opposite side of field or marking an opponent and now sprints toward his/her goal; TC may have been traveling side-to-side while marking an opponent and now moves toward his/her goal.) • Field positioning. TC often cuts wide to give teammate with the ball a passing option; TC attempts to beat a defender using body fake, dodge, speed or combination to remain open for a pass. • Communication. TC tells teammate with the ball that he/she is open to receive a pass, if needed. TC continues to communicate if a defender positions him/herself between ball and TC.
	Level 2 (Unacceptable) TC cannot consistently adjust when team transitions from defense to offense. TC adjusts using some of the following skills but is not consistent each time and consequently, is often out of position to be effective in any manner (in a game of at least 7 v. 7 of equal or near-equal teammates and competitors). Teammates never use TC during the transition plays, or even notice TC, because TC is behind the play when teammates quickly transition using an attacking speed: • Quick moves. TC changes speed and direction, as needed. (Examples: TC might have been jogging to move with the ball on opposite side of field or marking an opponent and now sprints toward his/her goal; TC may have been traveling side-to-side while marking an opponent and now moves toward his/her goal.) • Field positioning. TC often cuts wide to give teammate with the ball a passing option. TC attempts to beat a defender using body fake, dodge, speed or combination to remain open for a pass. • Communication. TC tells teammate with the ball that he/she is open to receive a pass, if needed. TC continues to communicate if a defender positions him/herself between ball and TC.
	Level 1 (Unacceptable) TC can't perform the following skills at game speed in the authentic environment (in a game of at least 3 v. 3 of teammates and competitors of equal or near-equal skill and tactical performance). The TC must play in a modified game at a slower speed in order to attempt to perform the skills. Sometimes in the modified game the TC can perform the skills and sometimes there are errors: • Quick moves. TC changes speed and direction, as needed. (Examples: TC might have been jogging to move with the ball on opposite side of field or marking an opponent and now sprints toward his/her goal; TC may have been traveling side-to-side while marking an opponent and now moves toward his/her goal.) • Field positioning. TC often cuts wide to give teammate with the ball a passing option; TC attempts to beat a defender using body fake, dodge, speed or combination to remain open for a pass. • Communication. TC tells teammate with the ball that he/she is open to receive a pass, if needed. TC continues to communicate if a defender positions him/herself between ball and TC.
	Level 0 (Unacceptable) TC does not attempt to perform the following skills in the authentic environment at game speed or in a modified game at a slower speed (game is of at least 3 v. 3 and competitors are of equal or near-equal skill and tactical performance): • Quick moves. TC changes speed and direction, as needed. (Examples: TC might have been jogging to move with the ball on opposite side of field or marking an opponent and now sprints toward his/her goal; TC may have been traveling side-to-side while marking an opponent and now moves toward his/her goal.) • Field positioning. TC often cuts wide to give teammate with the ball a passing option; TC attempts to beat a defender using body fake, dodge, speed or combination to remain open for a pass. • Communication. TC tells teammate with the ball that he/she is open to receive a pass, if needed. TC continues to communicate if a defender positions him/herself between ball and TC.

Invasion Sports Skill and Performance Concepts Assignment Data Table

Provided by Department of Kinesiology, Towson University

DATA TABLE FOR SKILLS (MINIMAL LEVEL OF ACCEPTABLE PERFORMANCE: LEVEL 3 ACCEPTABLE)

Soccer	Year	N	% TCs Unacceptable	% TCs Acceptable	% TCs Target
Kicking (Element 2.1)	07-08	21	4.76% (1/21)	23.81% (5/21)	71.43% (15/21)
	08-09	27	0% (0/27)	40.74% (11/27)	59.26% (16/27)
	09-10	19	10.53% (2/19)	21.05% (4/19)	68.42% (13/19)
			4.48% (3/67)	29.85% (20/67)	65.67% (44/67)
Trapping (Element 2.1)	07-08	21	9.52% (2/21)	19.05% (4/21)	71.43% (15/21)
	08-09	27	11.11% (3/27)	40.74% (11/27)	48.15% (13/27)
	09-10	19	15.79% (3/19)	31.58% (6/19)	52.63% (10/19)
			11.94% (8/67)	31.34% (21/67)	56.72% (38/67)
Dribbling (Element 2.1)	07-08	21	19.05% (4/21)	19.05% (4/21)	61.90% (13/21)
	08-09	27	7.41% (2/27)	37.04% (10/27)	55.56% (15/27)
	09-10	19	15.79% (3/19)	21.05% (4/19)	63.16% (12/19)
			13.43% (9/67)	26.87% (18/67)	59.70% (40/67)

Lacrosse	Year	N	% TCs Unacceptable	% TCs Acceptable	% TCs Target
Throwing (Element 2.1)	07-08	21	4.76% (1/21)	9.52% (2/21)	85.71% (18/21)
	08-09	26	3.85% (1/26)	23.08% (6/26)	73.08% (19/26)
	09-10	20	5% (1/20)	35% (7/20)	60% (12/20)
			4.48% (3/67)	22.39% (15/67)	73.13% (49/67)
Catching (Element 2.1)	07-08	21	4.76% (1/21)	23.81% (5/21)	71.43% (15/21)
	08-09	26	0% (0/26)	30.77% (8/26)	69.23% (18/26)
	09-10	20	5% (1/20)	40% (8/20)	55% (11/20)
			2.99% (2/67)	31.34% (21/67)	65.67% (44/67)
Cradling (Element 2.1)	07-08	21	4.76% (1/21)	9.52% (2/21)	85.71% (18/21)
	08-09	26	0% (0/26)	30.77% (8/26)	69.23% (18/26)
	09-10	20	0% (0/20)	45% (9/20)	55% (11/20)
			1.49% (1/67)	28.36% (19/67)	70.15% (47/67)

DATA TABLE FOR PERFORMANCE CONCEPTS
(MINIMAL LEVEL OF ACCEPTABLE PERFORMANCE: LEVEL 3 ACCEPTABLE)

Performance Concept	Year	N	% TCs Unacceptable	% TCs Acceptable	% TCs Target
Guard/Mark (Element 2.3)	07-08	21	4.76% (1/21)	9.52% (2/21)	85.71% (18/21)
	08-09	26	3.85% (0/26)	15.38% (4/26)	84.62% (22/26)
	09-10	20	0% (0/20)	10% (2/20)	90% (18/20)
			1.49% (1/67)	11.94% (8/67)	86.57% (58/67)
Adjust (Element 2.3)	07-08	21	4.76% (1/21)	28.57% (6/21)	66.67% (14/21)
	08-09	27	3.70% (1/27)	11.11% (3/27)	85.19% (23/27)
	09-10	19	0% (0/19)	21.05% (4/19)	78.95% (15/19)
			2.99% (2/67)	19.40% (13/67)	77.61% (52/67)

APPENDIX C:
NCATE PROGRAM REPORT PREPARATION FOR INITIAL LICENSURE

Appendix C provides information related to the program report preparation and submission process for NASPE/NCATE national recognition. This section can be useful in addressing specific questions for program report compilers or helpful in guiding programs new to the NASPE/NCATE process in seeking Specialized Professional Association (SPA) recognition. A complete repository of guidelines, resources, archived webinars, associated documents and a list of frequently asked questions can be found at the NCATE website (http://www.ncate.org/).

For PETE programs undergoing NASPE/NCATE review, please note that, under the 2008 Initial standards, all elements must be met. Previously, programs could meet the standards holistically; that is, by meeting most of the outcomes under each standard. With the substantial reduction in the number of standards and elements in 2008, programs seeking NASPE/NCATE national recognition now must provide evidence of meeting each of the elements using no more than eight assessments.

A *note about program report preparation and submission for accreditation*: NASPE acknowledges that the accreditation process evolves and that guidelines can change, as research evidence drives theoretical or procedural changes or as technology advancements streamline submission processes. Those changes dictate that teacher preparation programs visit the NCATE Web site (www.ncate.org/) routinely for news, updates and changes that can occur with the SPA program report preparation or submission process.

What If You Are Writing an NCATE Report?

The program report's purpose is to show candidate success in meeting the NASPE standards and elements. As noted above, programs must provide evidence through six to eight assessments identified in the program report's Section IV, Evidence for Meeting Standards. A NASPE/NCATE assessment consists of a narrative statement, a description of the assignment provided to the candidates, the scoring guide, and a data table.

For easier submission and review, program report compilers should merge the assessment information into one attachment for each assessment submitted. That means placing the narrative, description of the assignment provided to the candidates, the scoring guide and a data table — in that order — all in one document and labeling it with the assessment number that it's intended to represent. Details regarding what content to address in the narrative are provided in this appendix.

The initial program report contains five sections, in addition to the cover sheet. The cover sheet is where the program report compiler provides essential information about the program and provides documentation on achieving the 80 percent minimum pass rate on the required state examination (if one exists). Note: Check NCATE's Web site for exceptions to this reporting requirement.

Section I, Context, is where the program report compiler provides contextual information about the state, institution and unit policies that can affect the PETE program. The five specific statements to address in Section I:

1. Description of state and institutional policies. Clarify the program's ability to implement NASPE standards relative to specific state and/or institutional policies and practices.

2. Description of field and clinical experiences. Provide a narrative with details regarding types of

settings, types of experiences, duration of experiences, site selection criteria and factors used to determine selection and training of clinical teachers and university supervisors.

3. Program admission, retention and exit criteria. This section addresses required GPAs and minimal grade requirements for targeted coursework.

4. Program relationship to unit conceptual framework. If the PETE program has a separate conceptual framework from the unit, explain how the unit and program frameworks align.

5. Program assessments and relationship to unit assessment system. Clarify how program assessments align with unit assessments.

Finally, three attachments must accompany Section I and must address the following:

1. PETE program of study.

2. Chart of program teacher candidates and completers (labeled as Attachment A).

3. Chart of PETE program faculty (labeled as Attachment B).

Section II, List of Assessments, is a one-page chart that provides the assessment name and type, and when it is administered in the program. Section II is often completed following faculty study and discussion regarding:

- Analysis of candidate knowledge, skills and dispositions, and program effectiveness.

- Identification of existing assessments and data that provide evidence that candidates meet the NASPE standards.

- Development of additional assessments and scoring guides that will provide data as evidence of candidate success and positive effects on student learning.

NCATE requires each program to submit a minimum of six assessments, but no more than eight. Assessments 1 –5 must target areas specified by NCATE. The sixth required assessment provides more evidence of meeting the initial standards, but NCATE leaves the type of assessment to the program's discretion. Programs may submit one or two additional assessments (Assessment 7 and/ or 8), but those are optional.

The types of assessments to be submitted in the program report are:

- Assessment 1: Licensure assessment or other content-based assessment.

- Assessment 2: Content knowledge in physical education.

- Assessment 3: Candidate ability to plan instruction.

- Assessment 4: Internship or clinical experiences.

- Assessment 5: Candidate effect on student learning.

- Assessment 6: Additional assessment that addresses NASPE standards.

- Assessments 7 & 8: Additional assessments that addresses NASPE standards (optional).

Section III, Relationship of Assessments to Standards, is a chart that aligns with Sections II and IV. The chart's purpose is to show the alignment of each assessment with the NASPE standard(s) and element(s) for which it is intended to provide evidence. As with Section II, this section is often completed following faculty discussion regarding which assessments will be targeted for program report submission and analysis and submitted as evidence. Again, the assessment must provide evidence of candidate success in meeting the NASPE standard(s).

Section IV, Evidence for Meeting Standards, forms the heart of the program report, containing the six to eight assessments (in numerical order) as stated in Section II. Each assessment includes four components bundled into one document and labeled by assessment number. The order and requirements are:

1. Narrative
   a. A brief description of the assessment and where it is administered in the program.
   b. A description of how the assignment aligns with NASPE standards and elements.
   c. A brief analysis of the findings.
   d. An interpretation of how the data provide evidence of meeting NASPE standards and elements.

2. Description of the assignment as provided to candidates
   a. Specifies details of the assignment and what candidates "must do" to complete the assignment successfully.
   b. Should include the same instructions that candidates receive.

3. Scoring Guide
   a. Should be aligned clearly with the assignment.
   b. Should differentiate among levels of proficiency on the assignment (e.g., unacceptable, acceptable, target).

4. Data Table
   a. Summarizes candidate proficiency on the assignment.
   b. Should be aligned with the assignment and scoring guide.

Common Problems in Preparing Section IV

One of the most common mistakes in report preparation occurs when one part of an assignment is identified as meeting multiple standards and elements and that one part is evaluated with just a single item on the scoring guide. Measuring multiple elements with one item is known as "co-mingling."

For example, a program submits a unit plan assignment as Assessment 3 in the report. At first glance, the assignment description, scoring guide and data table all appear to be aligned with one another and the NASPE standards and elements.

Upon closer scrutiny, though, it's clear that the instruction portion of the unit plan assignment is purported to align with Elements 3.1, 3.3, 3.5, 3.6, 4.1, and 4.2. Because the, assignment, scoring guide and data table are all in alignment, the scoring guide used to assess this portion of the assignment also targets all six elements.

Finally, the data table provides data that are used to support six different elements under two different standards. In such cases, it's difficult for the candidate, the instructor and program faculty to determine the extent to which the data reflect the candidate's ability to execute Element 3.3 (design and implement content that is aligned with lesson objectives) versus Element 4.2 (implement effective demonstrations, explanations and instructional cues and prompts to link physical activity concepts to appropriate learning experiences).

Programs should modify the assessment when assignment and scoring guide implementation result in commingled data that are used to offer evidence for multiple elements under any one or more standards. The modifications should provide data, following scoring of the assignment, that provide evidence for one element or as few elements as possible under any one standard. The resultant data then can serve to more accurately pinpoint candidate and program strengths and weaknesses. Program faculty and reviewers also can use the data to determine the extent to which candidates are meeting the NASPE standards.

Reviewing the example above might reveal that the description of the assignment provided to the candidates is well written and provides accurate and clear expectations. Therefore, the assignment should not be rewritten; instead, the modifications should focus on reducing the number of elements with which any one portion of the assignment is intended to align.

As an alternative, the scoring guide can be revised to offer multiple entries used to assess any one portion of the assignment. For example, the instruction portion of the assignment described above might best be assessed by at least two scoring guide entries. One entry would assess candidates' ability to plan for instruction that includes explanation, instructional cues and demonstration; this entry might align with Element 3.3. The second entry of the scoring guide would assess candidates' ability to deliver the explanation, instructional cues and demonstration with K-12 students; this entry might align with Element 4.2.

These data would provide specific criteria regarding how candidates plan and deliver instruction. Disaggregated data such as these may reveal that some candidates create exceptional plans but struggle when delivering the plans to K-12 students.

Section V, Use of Assessment Results to Improve Candidate and Program Performance, is the final section of the initial program report. Typically, this also is the final section that the program report compiler completes before submitting the report. In this section, the program report compiler indicates how faculty interpreted the data generated from implementing the six to eight assessments submitted in Section IV.

NCATE is clear that the program report compiler is not to restate narrative information provided for each assessment, including reiterating the brief analysis of the findings or interpretation of how data from any one assessment provide evidence for meeting a NASPE standard and element. Instead, the narrative for Section V should be focused on content knowledge; pedagogical and professional knowledge, skills and dispositions; and effects on K-12 student learning. Responses to the following should address each of those areas:

- Summarize principle findings from evidence (data).

- Provide faculty members' interpretations of the findings.

- Describe steps that the program has taken, after faculty interpretation, to improve teacher candidate and PETE program performance.

- Provide programmatic changes/improvements made, or proposed, based on faculty interpretation.

The NCATE PRS system, in which NASPE uploads the program reports for review, contains character and page limits that differ by program report section. Visit the NCATE Web site for specific requirements for each section and for the most current information.

A program that doesn't have assessments already in place for the NASPE/NCATE program review process should consider following these steps to determine assessments, generate data and write an initial program report:

- Determine as a faculty which assessments, if any, align with the unit requirements and the NASPE standards/elements. The process of reviewing current assessments for alignment with the standards/elements must be completed early in the process.

- Once that review is completed, the faculty can determine whether assessments need to be revised or created to provide convincing evidence that candidates meet the standards/elements. The program must provide this evidence by using only six to eight assessments, so it's advisable to use or develop assessments that can provide evidence for multiple standards.

- The program faculty will need time to implement the revised or new assessments, collect data and revise assessments as needed based on the data collected.

- When revised or new assessments are first implemented, no data exist for the faculty to analyze or interpret. Faculty might wish to use this time to write Section I of the program report and pre- pare responses to narrative questions 1 and 2 for each of the six to eight assessments.

- Once faculty members have reached agreement regarding the six to eight assessments that will be submitted as Section IV, the program report compiler may complete Section II.

- Following completion of Section II, the program complier should complete Section III to ensure that one or more of the six to eight assessments provides evidence for each NASPE element.

As assessments are administered to candidates and scored, data will become available for analysis and interpretation. Once faculty members have interpreted how data provide evidence for candidates' mastery of the standard and/or element, they can answer questions 3 and 4 in the narrative.

After collecting, analyzing and interpreting all assessment data, the faculty can discuss how these data collectively demonstrate program effectiveness. In addition, faculty members might discuss where program weaknesses exist and develop plans for addressing those weaknesses. This information will be used for writing Section V of the program report.

Response to Conditions and Revised Reports

If a program doesn't achieve national recognition, it must submit a "response to conditions" or a "revised report" within a specified timeframe. The type of program report response will depend on the NASPE program reviewers' decision. Typically, a program that receives national recognition with conditions would submit a Response to Conditions Report. When preparing a Response to Conditions Report, program compilers must address all the conditions that are listed in the National Recognition Report and must specify the actions taken in response to the conditions listed in Part A of the National Recognition Report.

When developing a revised program report, program compilers should address all concerns noted under each standard listed as "not met" or "met with conditions" in Part B, and should respond to comments provided in Parts C, D and F of the National Recognition Report. See the NCATE Web site for complete details on Response to Conditions or revised program reports. Program report compilers do not need to write responses to standards that are marked as "met".

From the Reviewer's Perspective

The NASPE/NCATE review process relies on the SPA to determine the extent to which a program provides evidence that teacher candidates meet the standards/elements and meet or achieve the NCATE 80% pass rate on the state licensure test (where one exists). As noted above, NASPE/NCATE considers a standard met when evidence shows that teacher candidates are meeting every element under the standard. National recognition is awarded when all the NASPE standards have been met and data for the state licensure test meet or exceed the NCATE 80% pass rate. As such, the program report submitted to NCATE for review is a focused document providing evidence that programs are ensuring that candidates meet the intent of the NASPE standards and elements.

In addition to reviewing state licensure test data, NCATE charges reviewers from each SPA to focus on determining whether the standards have been met. Reviewers for NASPE program reports acknowledge that many programs offer unique and valuable experiences that assist teacher candidates in becoming highly qualified physical educators. If a unique program experience required of all candidates aligns with a NASPE standard or element, and the evaluation process results in meaningful data, it might be worthwhile for use as a program report assessment. The program report's purpose is to provide assessments and data that demonstrate that candidates meet the NASPE standards and elements.

If a unique program experience doesn't align with a NASPE standard or element, or is not evaluated in a manner that provides data and evidence for the standard or element, the faculty should modify it or consider an alternative assessment for the program report.

Programs might have worthwhile assignments that are important for the development of effective teachers but are not specifically aligned with the NASPE standards or elements. Programs can continue to require these assignments, but should not submit them as providing evidence for meeting the NASPE standards. The NASPE review process is specific to the national standards and elements. Programs will have quality assessments that go beyond the standards and that meet their programs' needs. The intent of the review process is not to limit program assessment, but to ensure that the standards are measured.

Additional Information Useful in Preparing Assessments (Initial Preparation Programs)

Additional Information Related to Initial Standard 1 and Elements 1.1-1.5

NASPE reviewers for program reports review the evidence/data asserting that teacher candidates achieve the NCATE 80 percent pass rate requirement on the state licensure test (when required). If data are sufficient, according to the NCATE program report preparation guidelines, then reviewers acknowledge the program has achieved the requirement.

Program report compilers often cite the evidence from the Praxis II® Subject Tests for Physical Education and/or the state licensure test to support NASPE Standard 1, Content Knowledge.

NCATE guidelines for state licensure tests include the following:

- Must have 80 percent pass rate in the most recent annual reporting period for state licensure exam of content knowledge (programs with fewer than 10 candidates in the most current year base pass rate on the total of completers over three years; programs with fewer than 10 candidates over three years are exempt from the 80% pass rate requirement).

- Programs in states that do not mandate a licensure exam of content knowledge must substitute an alternative test that provides evidence of candidate content knowledge for physical education; the alternative test must be submitted in the NCATE program report as Assessment 1 (the comprehensive exam will be submitted as the assignment, and submitted in its entirety, rather than a select group of sample questions; the answer key will be submitted as the scoring guide). The data table should align with the narrative question 2, which indicates alignment of test with NASPE standards and elements.

- Sub-scores on content portion of test must be reported for most recent annual reporting period (NCATE provides information for accessing sub-score data from ETS for Praxis II tests at: http://www.ncate.org/institutions/PraxisIIDataStd1.asp?ch=37).

- Range or standard deviation must be reported for the most recent annual reporting period.

- The narrative (Question 2) must show how the test aligns with the NASPE Initial PETE Standard(s) and Element(s).

Additional Information Related to Initial Standard 2 and Elements 2.1-2.3:

Programs must make plans for accommodations and/or modifications for teacher candidates with documented disabilities. To avoid discrimination against those with disabilities, physical education teacher candidates with special needs are allowed and encouraged to use a variety of accommodations and/or modifications to demonstrate competent movement and performance concepts (modified/adapted equipment, augmented communication devices, multi-media devices, etc.) and fitness (weight training programs, exercise logs, etc.).

Assignments and/or program requirements related to Elements 2.1-2.3 can be bundled as one assessment to provide evidence for Standard 2. This bundle could be submitted as Assessment 2, 6, 7 or 8.

Additional Information Related to Initial Standard 3 and Elements 3.1-3.7:

Teacher candidates are expected to both plan and implement planned lessons with K-12 students. The planned lesson designed or created by the teacher candidate must be the one that is implemented when evidence is provided for Standard 3 and its elements.

Additional Information Related to Initial Standard 4 and Elements 4.1-4.6:

Teacher candidates are expected to both plan and implement plans with K-12 students. It is assumed that the plan designed or created by the teacher candidate is the one that is implemented when evidence is provided for Standard 4 or its elements.

FREQUENTLY ASKED QUESTIONS

NCATE Program Report Preparation

Where can program staff find the NCATE guidelines for program report preparation?

Find the general guidelines for preparing an NCATE program report at: http://www.ncate.org/institutions/GuidelinesPreparingReport.asp?ch=90.

When you refer to the "six to eight required assessments," how are you defining an assessment?

An assessment is an evaluated activity or requirement by which a program determines that a candidate has mastered the standards and their elements. However, for the purposes of the program report, one or more of the six-eight assessment "slots" may actually be addressed with an amalgamation of assessments and data. For additional information, go to www.ncate.org/programreview/guidelinesFAQ.asp?ch=90.

Does NCATE provide a comprehensive Web site of information program staff can use when preparing assessments, program reports and other materials for accreditation?

Yes, NCATE provides information program staff can use when writing program reports for any of the SPAs affiliated with NCATE. The Web site, Guidelines and Procedures for the NCATE Program Review, may be accessed at the following link: http://www.ncate.org/institutions/guidelinesProcedures.asp?ch=90.

Find additional resources for submitting reports at: http://www.ncate.org/institutions/resourcesNewPgm.asp?ch=90.

May we use the same assessment for more than one of the six to eight required assessments?

Yes, although you need to think carefully about how you allot your assessments. For example, a comprehensive evaluation of a candidate portfolio for the student teaching semester may include in-depth assessments of both content knowledge and lesson planning. In this case, one section of the portfolio might be cited as Assessment 2 (content knowledge) and another section of the portfolio might be cited as Assessment # (ability to plan instruction). See www.ncate.org/programreview/guidelinesFAQ.asp?ch=90.

May we use one assessment to provide evidence for meeting multiple standards and/or multiple elements?

Yes. In a similar manner addressed in the previous FAQ response, one assessment may address numerous standards and elements. For example, an intern evaluation submitted as Assessment 4 might provide evidence for candidates' ability to plan and teach K-12 students in a physical education environment (Standard 3) as well as evidence of candidates' ability to recognize the changing dynamics and make appropriate adjustments (Element 4.4).

Our program would like to use course grades or candidates' GPA data as evidence for content knowledge. Is this permissible, and if so are guidelines available detailing how to include the data in a program report?

Yes, you can use course grades and candidates' GPA data as evidence of content knowledge (Standards 1 and 2). NCATE has prepared a document that states the guidelines for using and documenting course grades as an assessment of candidate content knowledge. Find the document at: http://www.ncate.org/institutions/GuidelinesGrades.asp?ch=90.

Does NCATE provide guidelines for programs that must submit a revised report or Response to Conditions report?

Yes. Find guidelines for preparing a revised report at: http://www.ncate.org/institutions/ guidelinesRevisedPgmS08.asp?ch=90.

Find guidelines for preparing a Response to Conditions report at: http://www.ncate.org/institutions/guidelinesResponseConditionS08.asp?ch=90.

How much data must a program provide for each assessment when submitting an initial program report to NASPE/NCATE?

For full recognition, programs must submit data that represent two applications* of the assessment. That is, the assessment must be given and data collected at least two times. If an assessment is in a class that is offered every semester, then the two applications could be satisfied in one academic year. If the assessment is in a class that is offered once per year, then the two applications will take two academic years.

*When new standards are written, the data requirements are modified. Check NASPE's Web site for up-to-date information on phasing in the data requirements.

How much data must a program provide for each assessment when submitting a revised or Response to Conditions Report to NASPE/NCATE?

For a revised and Response to Conditions Report, data from one application of the assessment would be required for full recognition.

What other resources are available to assist with program report submission?

NCATE has created free mini-videos at: http://www.ncate.org/programreview/miniPRS_pr.asp?ch=37.

In addition, find free archived webinars, guidelines documents and examples at: http://www.ncate.org/public/resourcesNewPgm.asp?ch=4.

NCATE Electronic Submission Process

Is information available to help when submitting an NCATE program report and attachments using AIMS at the PRS Web site?

Yes, you can find additional information for both the program report compiler and the unit assessment coordinator at the following link under Report Submission Process: http://www.ncate.org/institutions/guidelinesProcedures.asp?ch=90.

In addition, NCATE provides mini-videos for use in submitting program reports. The mini-videos detail how to log on to AIMS, how to fill out each section of the program report and how to submit attachments. Access the list of mini-videos at: http://www.ncate.org/institutions/miniPRS.asp?ch=90.

NASPE Initial Standards

Can a program bundle the data for Elements 2.1, 2.2 and 2.3 when submitting an NCATE program report?

Yes, you may bundle data used as evidence for a standard. It's important that the bundle include not only the required NCATE information (narrative addressing the four questions, assignment, scoring guide and data table) but also all criteria used to evaluate teacher candidates. For example, it's likely that different scoring criteria might be used to provide evidence for Element 2.1 compared with scoring criteria for Element 2.2. As such, both scoring guides would need to be submitted for review in the program report.

Can data from a Webquest assignment that teacher candidates implement with their K-12 students be used as evidence for Element 3.7?

Yes. A Webquest is an inquiry-oriented lesson format in which most or all the information that learners work with comes from the Web (Retrieved April 25, 2009 from http://webquest.org/index.php).

Are examples of program reports available to review for guidance in writing a program report?

Yes. Find examples of program reports at the NCATE Web site: http://www.ncate.org/programreview/programReportSamples.asp?ch=37.

Our unit uses a common assessment for clinical experiences. Will that be a concern for the program review process?

Generic student teaching/internship evaluations (those used by all programs in a unit) will not necessarily provide direct evidence of meeting specific SPA standards. Faculty members have several options to ensure that these kinds of unit wide assessments are appropriate for SPA review. For example, program faculty could develop an addition (additional evaluation items) to a generic student teaching/internship evaluation that does evaluate the candidate on appropriate SPA standards. Faculty could also code elements in the unit wide assessment with the specific SPA standards that are addressed by the item and, in the narrative in Section IV for this assessment, provide a rationale for how these items are evaluated in practice to ensure that SPA standards are addressed. A third option is to use a SPA-specific assessment completed during a pre-student teaching practicum. Find additional assessment information at: http://www.ncate.org/institutions/guidelinesProcedures.asp?ch=90.

RESURCES

Published by the National Association for Sport and Physical Education:

Quality Physical Education Programs

Moving Into the Future: National Standards for Physical Education, 2nd Edition (2004)

National Standards & Guidelines for Physical Education Teacher Education (2009)

Quality Coaches, Quality Sports: National Standards for Athletic Coaches (2006)

Physical Activity for Children: A Statement of Guidelines for Children Ages 5-12, 2nd Edition (2003)

Concepts & Principles of Physical Education: What Every Student Needs to Know, 2nd Edition (2003)

On Your Mark, Get Set, Go!: A Guide for Beginning Physical Education Teachers (2004)

Coaching Issues & Dilemmas: Character Building Through Sport Participation (2003)

Teaching Games for Understanding in Physical Education and Sport (2003)

Physical Activity and Sport for the Secondary School Student, 5th Edition (2002)

Opportunity to Learn Standards

Opportunity to Learn Guidelines for Elementary School Physical Education (2009)

Opportunity to Learn Guidelines for Middle School Physical Education (2009)

Opportunity to Learn Guidelines for High School Physical Education (2009)

Appropriate Practices

Appropriate Practices in Movement Programs for Children Ages 3-5 (2009)

Appropriate Instructional Practice Guidelines for Elementary School Physical Education (2009)

Appropriate Instructional Practice Guidelines for Middle School Physical Education (2009)

Appropriate Instructional Practice Guidelines for High School Physical Education (2009)

Appropriate Instructional Practice Guidelines for Higher Education Physical Activity Programs (2009)

Assessment Series

Assessing and Improving Fitness in Elementary Physical Education (2008)

Assessing Concepts: Secondary Biomechanics (2004)

Assessing Student Outcomes in Sport Education (2003)

Assessment in Outdoor Adventure Physical Education (2003)

Authentic Assessment of Physical Activity for High School Students (2002)

Elementary Heart Health: Lessons and Assessment (2001)

Creating Rubrics for Physical Education (2000)

Standards-Based Assessment of Student Learning: A Comprehensive Approach (1999)

 Order online at www.naspeinfo.org or call 1-800-321-0789

Shipping and handling additional.

National Association for Sport and Physical Education, an association of the American Alliance for Health, Physical Education, Recreation, and Dance (AAHPERD)

1900 Association Drive, Reston, VA 20191, naspe@aahperd.org, 703-476-3410, 703-472-8316 (fax)